WORK

Diva

how to climb the corporate ladder
without selling your soul

WORK

Diva

how to climb the corporate ladder
without selling your soul

KIM MEREDITH

Published by Oshun Books
an imprint of Random House Struik (Pty) Ltd
Company Reg. No. 1966/003153/07
80 McKenzie Street, Cape Town, 8001
PO Box 1144, Cape Town, 8000, South Africa

www.oshunbooks.co.za

First published 2009

1 3 5 7 9 10 8 6 4 2

Publication © Oshun Books 2009
Text © Kim Meredith 2009

'Ten Tips for Meeting with Mr Big' by Chrissy Scivicque.
Used by permission of Chrissy Scivicque of OfficeArrow.com
'Because I'm Not a Man' by Riley Klein. Used by permission of www.howtodothings.com
'The Whole of the Moon', music by Michael Scott © Warner/Chappel Music Ltd
– Administered by Gallo Music Publishers

Cover photograph © iStockphoto/Patrick Robbins

PUBLISHER: Marlene Fryer
MANAGING EDITOR: Ronel Richter-Herbert
PROOFREADER: Trish Myers-Smith
COVER DESIGNERS: Monique Oberholzer and Leigh Dyson
TEXT DESIGNER AND TYPESETTER: Monique Oberholzer
PRODUCTION MANAGER: Valerie Kömmer

Set in 11 pt on 15.5 pt Adobe Caslon

Reproduction by Hirt & Carter (Cape) (Pty) Ltd
Printed and bound by Paarl Print, Oosterland Street, Paarl, South Africa

ISBN 978 1 77020 083 8

For my father, John Gordon Meredith,
who taught me how to think

Contents

5 > RUNG 2: THE WORK DIVA'S SENSE OF STYLE

6 > RUNG 3: WORK DIVAS WHO STICK TOGETHER?

7 > RUNG 4: A WORK DIVA OF ART AND SUBSTANCE

8 > RUNG 5: THE WORK DIVA'S WICKED WAY WITH WORDS

9 > RUNG 6: BEING WITH THE POWERS THAT BE

10 > RUNG 7: WHEN SEX REARS ITS HEAD

11 > RUNG 8: FIVE WAYS TO FECK UP YOUR CAREER

12 > RUNG 9: BEFORE YOU REACH FOR THE TOP RUNG

13 > THE TOP RUNG: HOW NOT TO SELL YOUR SOUL

14 > THE WHOLE OF THE LADDER: STEP BACK AND REFLECT

Acknowledgements

There are so many people I need to thank for making this adventure into the Work Diva's world possible.

Firstly, and most importantly, my long-suffering husband Simon Carpenter, who feeds me and supports me from blunder to brilliance and back, and who maintains my faith in men, mankind and romantic love.

To all my friends – and I am blessed to have the most magnificent selection of friends – but especially the girls who have supported me in this endeavour: Barbara Edwards, Brenda Bensted-Smith, Karen Evans, Lorna Potgieter and Louise Chain. Not forgetting the boys: Allan Meyer, Ashley Marchment and Chris van der Walt.

A special word of thanks to Colleen Meredith, my mother, who is the kindest person in the whole wide world.

To the incredible people I have met in business, particularly my mentors and coaches: Bob Strain, David Black, Gary Harlow, Joan Joffe, Dr Karen Toombs, Nic Frangos, Nick Speare, Patrick Evans, Pauline Louw and Terry Dearling.

A huge thank you to Julie Purkis, aspiring Harley-Davidson owner, who ran the business far more competently than me while I wrote this book.

To Ronel Richter-Herbert and Marlene Fryer of Oshun Books for their gentle encouragement and for not destroying my spirit. Without this opportunity, I would not have been able to share my business scars with all the other Work Divas out there.

And, lastly, to the people mentioned in the book – all of whom are larger than life.

Introduction

Once upon a time there was a little girl who wasn't born with a silver spoon in her mouth. She did, though, have silver-lined dreams – dreams of making money and having a horse and getting kissed by a special boy. She wasn't born a princess and wasn't really sure how she would achieve her dreams, so she simply followed her heart, which told her that she belonged in the big bad world of business.

Just like in the fairy tales, the little girl's mother died when she was small, leaving her father with no money and three young children. But still she dreamt. She would wake her four-year-old brother in the middle of the night and tell him how she planned to fence off a park, charge people an entrance fee to bring their dogs to a grand dog show and then use the money to buy a horse. And on she dreamt. Twenty years went by, and still she woke various members of her family in the middle of the night to tell them how she was going to use the money recently released from her pension fund to start a business. And still she dreams. And still she wakes her family (now her husband) in the middle of the night.

Does this little girl live within you? Do you still have your dreams, even if they're somewhat modified? Do you still lie awake at night planning how you can take your career to dizzying heights, having swapped ponies for world travel along the way? If so, then this book is for you. This book is dedicated to the little girls within us adult women who still dare to dream their dreams.

But enough about dreams, and back to reality. I dislike business books – not what you want to hear from someone who's written one, I'm sure, but I find most of them terminally boring. There are, of course, a few notable exceptions, but business books, more often than not, fail to ignite the fire of the little-girl-with-big-dreams part of me – the part that keeps me awake at night with a head full of plots and plans. Perhaps this is the reason why so many of us women would rather sink our teeth into a juicy novel or gossipy magazine. Business books are generally written for men by men – with a passing or patronising reference to 'this works for women too' – or by scary, ball-busting, suit-wearing ultra-females who put the fear of god into us when we just look at the cover.

Was it really asking for too much expecting a book that helped real women address the real challenges they face as they climb the corporate ladder? How about finding a course that understood the needs of women wanting to become goddesses or divas in the corridors of power, rather than in the kitchen? All, naturally, without selling their souls. Well, it seemed that I *was* hoping for too much, and it was this simple realisation that encouraged me to create *Work Diva* and The Dealdiva™ programme. Spot the similarity between the two, dear diva?

There is a reason that the finest bowed instrument, the Stra*diva*rius, contains the word 'diva' – and, in my opinion, it has nothing to do with the last name of a famous family. According to www.wikipedia.com, 'The name "Stradivarius" has also become a superlative applied to designate excellence. To be called "the Stradivari" of any field is to be deemed the finest there is.'

There you – almost – have it! I wanted to find a word for the book and the programme that described the excellence in women but that also encapsulated their very essence and spirit. I hope you approve of the word I chose.

Work Diva and The Dealdiva™ are designed to give women all the support they may want or need to make the most of their potential – to climb that corporate ladder with confidence and style. It's time for women to acknowledge their dreams, to take charge of their work lives and to fulfil their ambitions. *Work Diva* is here to be the mentor and guide you've always wished for.

Kim Meredith
kimm@thedealmaker.com

Chapter 1

A VERY BRIEF *HER*STORY OF THE WORK DIVA

ARE YOU A DIVA OR A DOORMAT?

'There are only two types of women: goddesses and doormats.'
– *Pablo Picasso (Spanish painter; 1881–1973)*

If you do not know who Pablo Picasso is, please do not tell anyone. Google the name before you even begin reading the rest of this book, and find out. You cannot survive without a good general knowledge if you want to get ahead in business – or in life in general, in fact. Although I was flippant about business books in the Introduction, here's the bad news: If you want to be taken seriously in your career, you need to invest time in serious content.

In business, you are measured by your understanding of the world at large, the corporate world in general and your company in particular. Knowing who does what to whom in the latest Marian Keyes is not going to win you the big promotion or pay rise you are chasing. 'That's not fair,' you might moan. 'Men read golf magazines and that seems to help *them*!' No, it's not fair, but if you want a book about what's fair and how things *should* be in the world, then go back to reading that novel. If, however, you want a book that will help you to get ahead in the real – and very unfair – world of business as a woman, you've come to the right place. Sit back, kick off your shoes, grab a glass of wine and drive your career forward in comfort.

Back to Picasso: I happen to agree with his sentiment. My apologies to any devout feminists reading this book *(if you are a radical feminist, best give this book to someone else, as you won't find any male-bashing here)*, but just think about what Picasso said for a minute. Imagine this not as a sexist judgement, but rather as a way for women to view themselves. If you see yourself as a diva, you become a diva; if you see yourself as a doormat ... sorry for you. Nowhere in the world is your self-image as important as in the business world. People see you as you see yourself.

More women than I care to remember have told me that they have poor self-esteem because they get 'put down' by others – their mothers, sisters, fathers, ex-lovers, husbands, bosses, blah, blah, blah. Eleanor Roosevelt *(American humanitarian; 1884–1962)* said: 'Nobody can make you feel inferior without your permission.' Why have so many women allowed others to make them feel inferior? What happened? When did our self-esteem disappear down the drain with the dishwashing liquid? Let's take a quick peek at history to try to find an answer.

Only one hundred years ago, women in the Western world were not allowed to vote, go to university, hold down certain professional jobs or belong to most clubs. A woman's place was in the home – women were widely acknowledged to have no head for business, finance or law. As recently as 1950, women were still being *sold* in China, for heaven's sake. My friend Louise Chain, a brilliant executive coach in Australia, wrote an article recently about how, just fifty years ago, two women were told to forego their places in medical school because not enough male students had qualified for the next year – even though these women were at the top of their classes! A lot has changed in a very small space of time.

We owe a huge debt to our suffragette sisters, and all the other people – including many men – who fought for the rights of women. But with a history of being suppressed, repressed, subjugated, dominated and generally tyrannised, women are still battling to escape from the box in which they were kept for centuries.

Back to Picasso and Eleanor Roosevelt. Are you a goddess or a doormat? Do you give people permission to put you down? This needs to stop. Now. This book's purpose is to guide you through the minefield in which you find yourself and help you to become the Work Diva you have always dreamt of being.

THE GOOD, THE BAD AND THE VICTIM

'The greatest discovery of all time is that a person can change his future by merely changing his attitude.' – *Oprah Winfrey*
(American talk show host, media mogul and philanthropist; 1954–?)

There are a few stereotypes which people, particularly women, need to deal with: those within us and those outside us. We can change the way in which we see – and treat – ourselves, and we can even change the way we behave, but we can do very little to change the perceptions and behaviour of others. Accept this as the first rule of getting ahead in business and in life. The next step is to stop the blame. Stop being a victim. After centuries of real unfairness, it's time for women to take charge of their dreams, and damn the rest.

The world is *not* fair – people are born disabled or lose those they love; people who don't deserve it earn more than you, or will be promoted sooner than you. You can't change this, but what *can* you change? How about starting with a change in outlook? Nobody likes to be surrounded by the 'I'm so hard done by' specialist. You know *you're* guilty of some serious self-pity when

– the eyes of the person to whom you are whingeing glaze over, or they stop responding to you and your tale of woe, or
– your friends and family seem to be avoiding you.

We all fall into this little routine from time to time, but if you find yourself grousing *a lot*, well, then it's time for a change.

Quick check: How often do you find yourself blaming something, or someone, other than your attitude for your problems? If you blame external factors regularly, you may have a deep-rooted 'victim mentality' and not even realise it. Blaming other people or even other forces (saying, for example, 'I'm so unlucky') is the single biggest indicator of a victim state of mind – and the quickest possible way to damage your career. Blaming others is the antichrist of success and can be identified with the continual whine of 'it's not fair'. If you use any of the following victim war cries, then I have bad news for you – you have become a casualty of the victim mindset:

- It's because I'm a woman/not a man/too young/too old.
- It's because I'm not pretty/sexy/thin/fat enough.
- It's because I'm black/white/not black enough/not white enough.
- It's because I'm (insert religion here).
- It's because he/she doesn't like/love/appreciate/notice me.
- It's because my mother/father didn't love me/abandoned me/beat me.
- It's because of apartheid/Black Economic Empowerment/the government/the colonialists/crime/poverty/…
- It's because I have such bad luck/bad karma/a difficult life.

The good news is that all the above woes can be cured! All you need is a change in outlook. Stop moaning and start *counting your blessings*. Just this one tiny adjustment to your mindset will change your view – and your life – forever.

Talking about changing attitudes and outlooks, it's time to have a long, hard close-up with a mirror. What is really 'good' and 'bad' about you? We all have both good and bad in us – call them positives and negatives, or yin and yang, or dark chocolate and light chocolate, or whatever. When I was seventeen, I sat down and wrote a list of all the things I liked and disliked about myself – on the inside and the outside. I rediscovered this list a while back and realised that, over the years, I have, without even trying, overcome many of my 'bads'. I don't know what wisdom was guiding me. I would love to say that it was some kind of clever awareness on my part, but this would not be the truth. I think that by simply writing the stuff down, my super-conscious dealt with it at a much wiser level than I can pretend to control.

For example, as a teenager I was racked with jealousy. I was jealous of the other girls' (I was at an all-girls' school) clothes, boyfriends, money, mothers … you name it. I don't think there is any of this jealousy in me today.

What happened? By simply acknowledging them, my super-conscious (call it unconscious if you prefer) has been quietly working on my 'bads', to the point where most of these traits have disappeared. When I reread my list after all these years, I was mortified to see how negatively I had thought of myself – I would never be *that* unkind to myself now – but I was also delighted that seventeen-year-old me had been brave enough to write it.

It's never too late to write your own list. Be honest, and then file the list away for posterity. Don't dwell on the 'bads' – let them go. Just be the best of the 'good' you can.

I knew a fabulous woman, Sally, who was not a raving beauty. She was overweight and had a delightful little squint. Sally knew this, but she also knew that she was funny and sexy and hardworking, and that people, especially men, were attracted to her like bees to honey. It would have been so easy for her to listen to her brother, who was forever going on at her about her weight, or the men in her past who had let her go for being 'over the top', but Sassy Sally understood that people loved her for who she was. So, instead of trying to eradicate these 'bads', which existed in the minds of others, she focused on her strengths and polished them up to a shine. She listened to her inner cheerleader and, as a result, was simply ravishing.

The moral of this story? Stop waiting for others to change their view of you, as it ain't gonna happen. Stop blaming everyone and everything. Start listening to *your* inner cheerleader. Recognise the 'bads', file these away, and focus on making the most of your 'good'. It's time to be brave and write your list. Below are a few ideas you can use for your list, but be sure to use your own words – this is, after all, *your* list. Focus only on those factors that you think are *really* 'good' or *really* 'bad' – exclude anything about which you don't feel strongly. It is important that you do *not* ask other people for their input. This is your private list over which only you must have control. Also, what you may see as a 'good', e.g. manipulative, someone else may see as a 'bad'.

Take your time drawing up your list – it is a really, really important exercise – and then file it away with a note saying, 'Not to be looked at again until [put down a date about five to ten years ahead]'.

THE GOOD AND THE BAD WORKOUT

> 'How desperately difficult it is to be honest with oneself. It is much easier to be honest with other people.'
> – *Edward Frederic Benson (American author; 1867–1940)*

GOOD ME	BAD ME
Pretty/thin/tall/petite/young/mature	Plain/fat/tall/short/old/childish
Attractive/sexy/sassy/great in bed	Unattractive/dowdy/take in bed
Stylish/fashionable/individualistic/elegant	No dress or make-up sense or interest/ slave to fashion/slob
Good hair/teeth/breasts/legs	Bad hair/teeth/feet/breath
Fun/funny/light-hearted/serious/ interested/make an effort	Bored/flippant/serious/uninformed/ expect others to make the effort
Healthy/fit/adventurous/cautious	Unhealthy/lazy/scaredy cat
Kind/share/generous/give praise/keep secrets/honest/diplomatic	Nasty/selfish/mean/critical/gossipmonger/ dishonest/tactless
Passionate/committed/go out on a limb/ take risks	Dispassionate/can't commit/take risks
Loving/sharing/forgiving/nurturing	Cold/judgemental/blaming/inflexible/ smothering/jealous
Clean living/good values/flexible	Don't know what I want or who I am/ opinionated/morally reprehensible
Don't drink/smoke/take drugs	Drink too much/glutton/addictive personality
Take charge of my life/accept and take responsibility/independent thinker	Victim/hard done by/blame/ co-dependent
Have responsibilities	Have rights

Chapter 2

BEFORE THE LADDER:
STEREOTYPES AND OTHER ANIMALS

DEFENDING THE CAVEMAN FROM MARS

'The emotional, sexual, and psychological stereotyping of females
begins when the doctor says, "It's a girl."'   *– Shirley Chisholm*
(American presidential candidate; 1924–2005)

Those of us who saw the play *Defending the Caveman* laughed like hyenas. The play, which had universal appeal (it was performed across the globe and in fifteen languages) was funny because it exaggerated gender stereotypes. The book *Men Are from Mars, Women Are from Venus* by Dr John Gray has the same effect. Now, far be it for me to make light of the venerable Dr Gray's work, but, in reality, gender stereotyping *should* be kept light. If you take it too seriously, you will allow it to negatively impact you or reduce you to victim mode. This makes a mockery of being a wonderful, wily, wilful woman.

How do we maintain our independence as women without falling into a stereotype? What is the fine line that divides independent women from the lunatic feminist fringe? Let's start with marriage. I got married, for the first time, when I was in my forties. Okay, I had been with the same man for thirteen years, but it was still a

9

massive step for me. The first question I faced, as a married woman, was whether or not I should take my husband's surname. Sure, like everyone else, I'd spent days signing my first name combined with my boyfriend's last name when I was in my early twenties, but I'd never really given the matter serious thought.

For the best part of twenty years I had been carving out my business identity and building my network, but if I had to start phoning people up and saying, 'Hi, it's Kim Carpenter here – I used to be Kim Meredith', (a) did I want to have to go through the explanation, and (b) why should I have to change my identity? Why shouldn't he change *his* name?

I was in a real quandary. I didn't want to sell out as a woman and simply adopt my husband's name just because society expected it of me. But neither did I want to send out the message that I wasn't really committed to my marriage. Societal norms and my Leo nature were at odds. Oh, what to do?

I did eventually change my name on all the legal documents, but decided to keep my maiden name as my 'trading name'.

What would you do? What *have* you done? Did you, or will you, lose your identity when you get married? Take his name, or don't, the decision is yours. But whatever you do, don't lose your identity in the process. It is all too easy to become someone's wife or mother or employee, but stay true to who you are and celebrate that special person that you are all the time. Stuff the stereotypes. But to what extent do they impact the equality game?

DO I NEED A PENIS OR A BIG STICK?

'The cry of equality pulls everyone down.' — *Iris Murdoch*
(Irish writer; 1919–1999)

I will mention the amazing people I am blessed to have in my life many times in this book. One of them is my friend Karen Evans, managing director of a sizeable property company. Karen is beauty-queen gorgeous, warm, feminine and strong. I asked her the other day what she attributed her success to in a male-dominated environment. She replied by saying, 'Funny, I've never thought of it that way. I've never considered myself a woman in a man's world. Maybe at an unconscious level I know that as a woman I need to box smarter and work harder, but I've always just got on with it and done the very best I can. I make sure that I always give outstanding service to my customers, so they trust me and stay with me. It's not really a man vs woman thing.' Dumb question to ask a very smart woman, Kim.

If you find yourself sprouting forth the immortal words, 'It's because I'm not a man,' then go back to the previous chapter and spend an honest moment with yourself about having a victim frame of mind. If you, for more than one minute, allow yourself to use the excuse 'It's because I'm a woman,' you need to put this mindset on your 'bad' list and file it away. Samuel Johnson *(English author and writer of the first dictionary; 1709–1784)* said, 'Nature has given women so much power that the law has very wisely given them little.' Johnson was reputedly a misogynist, so what did he know about women that you have forgotten? Reclaim that power, princess!

That said, I was having lunch recently with a friend of mine, Ashley Marchment, when we bumped into an ex-colleague of my husband. After his lunch guest had left, the ex-colleague, Desmond, pulled up a chair to have a drink with Ashley and me. I introduced Ashley as 'one of the country's top sales coaches', and explained that he now focused on corporate culture transformation. Desmond then asked what I was 'doing'. I said that my company works with executives and, using coaching-based sales and negotiation interventions, we improve the profitability and increase the market share of organisations. Desmond had recently joined a large consulting company, and he began to describe to us the problems this company was having with its sales approach. He totally ignored that this was my area of expertise, and addressed all his questions and concerns to Ashley. I was astounded.

After Desmond left, I asked Ashley why he thought Desmond had ignored me and focused on him. Was it because I lacked business presence, or because I had not presented my company in the right light? Should I have told Desmond that I was, in fact, the managing director of my own damn organisation, or done a harder sell? Was it because I had introduced Ashley as a guru, or was it because Ashley's a *man*?

Ashley, with his infinite wisdom, said, 'Kim, you did everything right. The problem is, Desmond will never see you in any light other than as Simon's wife, no matter what you achieve in your life.' This threw me. I spent the whole evening thinking about it. Simon came home from work, took one look at my face and asked what was wrong. I told him that I was 'working through something', and he did what any good husband does and left me to my own devices.

Only the next morning was I ready to tell him about my interaction with Desmond and how it had irritated me. 'What can you learn from it?' he asked. I think the lesson was this – no matter how hard you work or how high you rise in the ranks of the business world, there will always be those who put you in a box marked 'Woman: cook, clean, make home and babies'. There is nothing you can do to change the perceptions of people like Desmond, but what you *can* do – and what I did – is to pick yourself up, dust yourself off and refuse to give up. Remember what Eleanor Roosevelt said about giving others permission to make you feel inferior? For that moment, I had given a small-minded person power over me – I had cared what Desmond thought. It can happen easily, so be on your guard and give yourself a good talking-to when you catch yourself saying, 'It's because I'm not a man!'

Seriously, though, if I had a dollar for every time I have been put down, ignored or otherwise diminished by others – usually men, but not always – I would be as rich as Madonna. But Madonna has also been put down and ignored, no doubt about it. And, like Madonna, I don't think we should let this stop us from being the very best we can be. We should take a leaf out of Beauty Queen Karen's book and 'just get on with it'. Bugger the professional put-downers.

IF WOMEN HAD A PENIS FOR A DAY

'See, the problem is that God gives men a brain and a penis, and only enough blood to run one at a time.'   – *Robin Williams*
                    (American actor and comedian; 1951–?)

Have you ever wondered what it would be like to be a man, even if only for a day? Whenever I've encountered obstacles in business that I'm sure only women have to face, this notion has certainly crossed my mind. In researching whether other women entertained similar thoughts, I wasn't able to find much in the way of sensible input, but I did come across this amusing little 'survey' on www.jokeroo.com, the origins of which I was unable to find. Women were asked: 'What would you do if you woke up and had a penis for a day?' Here are a few of their actual responses:

- I would write my name in the snow.
- I would find my ex-boyfriend, go to bed with him and tell him to roll over and try something new.
- I could grab myself in public and not be embarrassed.
- I would not lift the lid on the toilet seat while peeing.
- I would speed to the hospital and have it surgically removed.
- I would treat women better with it.
- Demonstrate to my husband and my two sons that it is possible to hit the water and not pee all over everything.
- Pin my husband down and slap him in the face with it.
- Stand up and jump up and down and watch it swing all around.
- See how many doughnuts I could carry with it.
- Check out my boyfriend's gag reflexes.

While I've never thought about being a man in quite this context, I do rather fancy the doughnut idea! What I want to know is, what would *you* do? Knowing what you know about gender stereotypes, would you really behave differently, or would you just have a bit of fun with your penis for the day? I would opt for the fun myself!

SOME ARE MORE EQUAL THAN OTHERS

> 'All animals are equal but some animals are more equal than others.'
> – *George Orwell (English author and satirist; 1903–1950)*

So how different are men and women really, apart from the obvious physiological differences? Let's take a look at a few pros and cons in the context of the Work Diva.

Ten reasons why being a woman in business is a disadvantage

1. Men are the incumbent power holders. They hold down the big jobs and are in positions of power, they make the key decisions – and they seem to have a private club from which women are excluded.

2. Men are seldom oversensitive and are less emotional than women in business – they do not take things personally.

3. Men are more prepared to put their jobs first, so their professional commitment is perceived to be greater than that of women, particularly women with children.

4. There are still plenty of men around who are chauvinists and misogynists, and thus women are diminished or not taken seriously in the workplace – they should, after all, be barefoot and pregnant in the kitchen!

5. Women who compete directly with men are seen to be (and often are) hard-core, ball-busting, *über*-bitches (think about it – do you prefer having a male or a female boss?).

6. Men are far more ready to invest in themselves to elevate their levels of business knowledge and skill – they attend courses and read the business books, financial magazines and trade journals, while women are busy lamenting, 'I don't understand all this financial stuff,' or 'I'm no good with numbers.'

7. Men who are confident are seen as confident, whereas women who are confident are seen as aggressive and pushy.

8. Men *are* generally more confident in the business environment than women – many women are only first- or second-generation career girls, whereas men have been doing this for millennia.

9. Women are seen as the weaker sex, and thus can't possibly be capable of driving business deals as well as a man (the latter, unfortunately, is often true), besides which, women don't understand 'the financial stuff'.

10. The glass ceiling is a reality – women have to not only work harder, but also smarter, to be taken seriously in the business world.

Eleven reasons why being a woman in business is an advantage

1. There is an old adage that women don't make good soldiers, but when they do become soldiers, they are far more ruthless and fearless than their male counterparts. Think Boudica, the Amazons, Catherine the Great or Joan of Arc. The same applies in business. Think Joan Joffe, Cynthia Carroll, Maria Ramos – even Dolly Parton. Work Divas one and all.

2. Women have 'feminine wiles' – they are generally more intuitive, cunning and manipulative than men (this is the 'nature' to which Samuel Johnson referred). The problem is that most women don't trust or use their feminine wiles enough in the workplace. Men class tears as feminine wiles, and perhaps they are?

3. The fact that there are still plenty of men around who are chauvinists is a massive plus for women – these men are especially susceptible to female wiles. They are so wonderfully easy to read, distract, manipulate …

4. Not all women are destined for motherhood. When a woman puts her career first, she is usually more committed than most men would ever be – she will happily work long hours, sacrifice her private time and be prepared to do work that is well beneath her capabilities to get ahead.

5. Because women are typically less confident in the business world than men, they are prepared to work much harder and with greater dedication to prove themselves.

6. Women can multitask and, with their tendency to pay greater attention to the detail, they can handle more assignments, do them all at the same time and deliver them to the highest of standards.

7. Women are less driven by ego and testosterone than men, and are thus far more willing to start at the bottom, perform menial tasks and let others take the credit, making them the preferred members of a team.

8. When it comes to human relations, women are perceptive, insightful and flexible, which is why they are better at dealing with conflict and effecting change in the work environment.

9. Women are far more open and approachable than men. They are also willing to share their feelings and listen to the concerns of others, which makes them superior communicators and ideal consultants and counsellors.
10. Being the sensitive sex, women are better able to read the subtleties and nuances of situations. They pick up details like body language, ulterior motives, hidden agendas and vibes that men tend to miss.
11. 'Sex sells' goes the saying, and, like it or not, it is true. Women who celebrate their sexuality (remember Sassy Sally?) have men by the short and curlies. This does not mean actually *having* sex with anyone or behaving in an overtly sexual manner – it's about being confident in and celebrating your femininity. If you are not comfortable with innuendo, then steer clear, but don't be jealous or critical of those women who understand the fine art of flirtation.

I was writing these lists while sitting around a fire with my man Simon and some very dear friends of ours at a private game lodge on Welgevonden in the Waterberg. When I asked the men in the group what they thought a woman's greatest advantage was in business, they all simultaneously yelled, 'Tits!' Maybe this should be item 12. Chauvinist pigs!

What can you do to overcome the disadvantages and maximise the advantages of being a woman? Firstly, recognise that the items above are both perceptions and generalisations. Accept them as truths or recognise them to be stereotypes – your call. But whether truths or stereotypes, 'know thy enemy', as Sun Tzu said *(Chinese general; c. 544–496 BC)*. Why not use these twenty-one items to help you achieve your goal of being a truly accomplished Work Diva?

Chapter 3

BENEATH THE LADDER:
WORK DIVA OR WONDER MOM?

MOTHERHOOD AND APPLE PIE

'As far as the court was concerned, I was a wicked career woman who put her children second. It was utter rubbish: I simply wanted to have both.' — *Karen Martin (British businesswoman and mother, after losing custody of her children in 2008)*

In Lucia van der Post's wonderful book *Things I Wish My Mother Had Told Me*, she writes about being both a devoted mother and a career professional. Much to my surprise, she holds a view with which I have always secretly agreed. She says that it is not possible to achieve dizzying success in both. You really do need to choose. Does this come as a surprise to you? Did those magazine articles have you believing that you could be the brilliant mother *and* the brilliant businesswoman? You can, but it's highly unlikely to happen at the same time. It's about *balance*.

We all have the potential to be supermodels, right, but in reality only a tiny fraction of the population will actually become supermodels. The same applies to being the perfect mother *and* the Work Diva. Only a minute handful of women will get it right. For the mere mortals amongst us, stop believing the magazines that say you *can* have it all, and choose the one you want at that moment in time. You do not, of course, *have* to choose – you can try to be supermom *and* career goddess – but remember the odds are similar to those of becoming a supermodel. If you can have only one, which should you choose?

Here's a conundrum to help you with your decision: Imagine that you have a strict deadline for an important project at the office. The deadline can't be extended, and if you can get a quality project in on time, you'll be the front-runner for the promotion for which you've been working very hard. Your boss had concerns about giving you the project, as he knows you have two small children. You assured him that you would not let him down.

With just one week to go to deadline, you get a call from the nursery school saying that your younger child has found and eaten snail poison and has been rushed to hospital. You dash to the hospital, to find that he is a very sick little boy. The doctors are concerned that, although his stomach has been pumped, serious side effects may yet emerge. They advise you to stay at his bedside for the next few days, as he needs constant support and care. He does not want his daddy, only you. You will not be able to complete the project if you are away from the office.

What do you do? It's really quite an easy choice, isn't it? Rather than trying to be brilliant at both and ending up being mediocre or a failure, how about giving one your full attention and putting the other on the back burner for a while? Don't forget, though, to treat those articles that suggest 'if you aren't having it all you're a lousy disappointment' with the contempt they deserve.

If you want meaningful input to help you with your 'children vs career' decision, you need to do two things: talk and read. Talk to women who have chosen to put their children first, and talk to women who have not had children. Talk to the women who are trying to balance motherhood with a career. And talk to men about their perceptions of 'mothers in business'. Then read, and read some more. Read books, research papers, the internet – anything where decent analysis or study has been conducted. You may notice that I haven't listed magazines here. While some articles can be very good, bear in mind that magazines (and newspapers) do not usually give more than a few pages to any story, due to space constraints. This means no in-depth analysis.

If you are secretly saying, 'Well, short articles suit me just fine,' all I can say is that you would be basing one of your most important life decisions on a snapshot view of the subject. Read the short articles by all means, but support these with real books, detailed research and actual conversations.

At the end of the day, the more insight you have, the more comfortable you will be making the decision that is right for you.

ON HAVING IT ALL

'That's the key to having it all: stop expecting it to look like what you thought it was going to look like.' — *Cindy Chupack*
(American writer/producer of Sex and the City; *1965–?)*

I recently read a review of Dr Linda Friedland's book *Having It All* in an edition of *Get It* magazine (this is where magazines are terribly useful and come into their own). Dr Linda Friedland, a very attractive South African–born medical doctor, speaker and businesswoman, has five children *and* a successful career. The review contained an extract from the book, which read, 'I believe that juggling motherhood and a career is entirely possible – you *can* have it all. For the vast majority of women who choose – and *want* – to do both, the important thing is not to have to choose one over the other, but to integrate them while still ensuring that you can take care of yourself.'

I was intrigued – had Dr Linda found some secret way of balancing supermom with career diva? She sure had! To her credit, she does mention that she has a supportive husband, supportive and independent kids, and 'two amazing full-time housekeepers and a fantastic au pair'. There – you, too, now know the secret!

As you've probably read between the lines, I'm a wee bit sceptical of a woman giving advice to us lesser mortals when she appears to be doing so from a position of having all the possible advantages (sort of like a supermodel giving diet tips).

But there does seem to be some good, self-affirming stuff in the book, so don't toss the baby out with the bath water. You may want to include it in your research to give you an alternative view.

To my mind, there is absolutely no shame in being both the wonderful mother and the career goddess – *one at a time*. Choose the one about which you are passionate at that moment in your life and, when it comes to the other, accept that you will just have to do the best you can for the time being. If you choose your career over your children, you are likely to feel huge guilt, so make sure you do everything in your power to give your kids the infrastructure and support they need in your absence. If you can't afford this, you have your answer.

One question: Where does looking after *you* come into all of this? It is essential that you make (and take) the time to invest in yourself – your physical, sexual and spiritual well-being (which means your health, appearance, love life, sex life, friends, family, social life, etc.). Maybe, just maybe, you need to balance *three* things: your kids, your career *and* your self. I have a view, with which many people are bound to disagree, that you should look after *you* first. If you are an exhausted, tattered and worn-out wreck, you're not going to be of much use to your kids or your company. I'm not suggesting that you should spend the most *time* on yourself – just that you should look after your own well-being *first* and then invest in all of the other demands being made on you.

Good luck with all the balancing, but I have no doubt that, as an aspirant Work Diva, you can do it!

TO BREED OR NOT TO BREED

> 'I've yet to be on a campus where most women weren't worrying
> about some aspect of combining marriage, children and a career.'
> – *Gloria Steinem (American feminist and journalist; 1934–?)*

Let's step back for a moment and have a look at the bigger picture. Women today – well, the liberated ones, anyhow – have the choice of whether or not to have children in the first place. This needs to be an *active* decision that every self-actualised woman makes – not something we just 'do' as part of our life path. Not all women want children, while others may be desperate to have kids. We need to respect each other's individual choices, which can be very difficult when someone else's decisions conflict with every fibre of your own value system. Why do I make this last, seemingly obvious, statement? Well, the 'Moms' club' and the 'Non-breeders'.

I was at a breakfast a few years ago with my beautiful friend Karen Evans. It was a 'women-only' launch of the BMW 6 Series. Each table seated about ten women, most of whom did not know each other. Nosey by nature, I started asking the other women questions about their lives, and quickly discovered that the majority at our table had been invited to the event because their husbands had bought them BMWs. I was appalled – how could these women allow their husbands to buy them cars? I was distressed – they had sold out their independence! When I asked the women *why* they hadn't bought their own cars, the table quickly divided into two camps. You guessed it: 'the 'Moms' club' and the 'Non-breeders'. Only three or so women had bought their own cars – and they were all childless. I had an 'aha' moment, but the moms were by now hostile towards Karen, an innocent bystander, and me.

As our discussions veered towards the violent, I realised that I viewed women who had chosen not only to have children, but to relinquish their earning power to their husbands – or ex-husbands, in a couple of cases – with disdain. And I realised that they saw career girls, like Karen and me, as a threat. We were the women with whom their husbands had interesting conversations and saw in their best clothes with perfect make-up. We were never covered in baby puke or Koki pen. They did not see us *in* the bath with screaming toddlers ('It's easier to bath three small kids that way,' my sister Shelley Lotriet explained to me). The battle lines were drawn, but I backed down. I realised that I was judging these mothers for their choices, just as they were judging me for mine. I could not control their views, but I sure could control my own.

The point of what I'm saying is that we do not always support the decisions of other women when their choices differ from our own. We are not the 'sisterhood' men believe us to be – but more on this later. Women already face stereotypes and inequality perpetuated by both sexes, so when it comes to being the Work Diva, you need to be 100 per cent sure of your choice to have children, and then whether you put your children or your career first. Again, make the decision that is right for *you*.

Something to watch out for: If you do not have children, or if you decide to put your career before your kids, avoid, at all costs, the temptation to mother your colleagues – or, heaven forbid, your boss. If you have a nurturing nature, bear in mind that there is a danger of confusing your role as a mother with what is expected of you as a business person. While everyone in the office may love you because they can run to you to tell you their problems while you stroke their hair and make them feel better, the powers that be may not see this as the primary quality they want in a rising superstar. Use your motherly powers to benefit the company as a whole, not just the individuals within the organisation.

ON YOUR MARKS, GET SET, GO!

> 'Children nowadays are tyrants. They contradict their parents, gobble their food and tyrannise their teachers.'   – *Socrates*
> *(Greek philosopher; c. 469–399 BC)*

And now for a bit of fun!

Are you ready to have kids? Ever thought about having children but aren't sure? Follow these fifteen simple tests before you decide to have children:

Test 1 – Preparing for ma/paternity

Women: To prepare for maternity, put on a dressing gown and stick a beanbag down the front. Leave it there for nine months. After nine months, remove 10 per cent of the beans.

Men: To prepare for paternity, go to local chemist, tip the contents of your wallet onto the counter and tell the pharmacist to help himself.
Then go to the supermarket. Arrange to have your salary paid directly to their head office. Go home. Pick up the newspaper and read it for the last time.

Test 2 – The wisdom of the uninitiated

Find a couple who are already parents and berate them about their methods of discipline, lack of patience, appallingly low tolerance levels and how they have allowed their children to run wild. Suggest ways in which they might improve their child's sleeping habits, toilet training, table manners and overall behaviour. Enjoy it. It will be the last time in your life that you will have all the answers.

Test 3 – The nights with baby

To discover how the nights will feel:

1. Walk around the living room from 19h00 to 22h00 carrying a wet bag weighing approximately four to six kilograms with a radio tuned to static (or some other obnoxious sound) at top volume.
2. At 22h00, put the bag down, set the alarm for midnight and go to sleep.
3. Get up at 00h00 and walk the bag around the living room until 01h00.
4. Set the alarm for 03h00.
5. As you can't get back to sleep, get up at 02h00 and make a cup of tea.
6. Go to bed at 02h40.
7. Get up again at 03h00 when the alarm goes off.
8. Sing songs in the dark until 04h00.
9. Set the alarm for 05h00. Get up when it goes off.
10. Make breakfast.

Keep this up for five years. Look cheerful.

Test 4 – Dressing baby

Dressing small children is not as easy at it seems.

1. Buy a live octopus and a string bag.
2. Attempt to put the octopus into the string bag so that none of the arms hang out.

Time allowed for this – all morning.

Test 5 – The family car

Forget the BMW and buy a practical five-door hatchback. And don't think that you can leave it out on the driveway spotless and shining. Family cars don't look like that.

1. Buy a chocolate ice cream cone and put it in the glove compartment. Leave it there.
2. Get a coin. Insert it in the CD player.
3. Take a family-size package of chocolate biscuits and mash them into the back seat.
4. Run a garden rake along both sides of the car.

There. Perfect!

Test 6 – Leaving the house with baby

Get ready to go out.

1. Wait.
2. Go out the front door.
3. Come in again.
4. Go out.
5. Come back in.
6. Go out again.
7. Walk down the front path/driveway.
8. Walk back up again.
9. Walk down the path again.
10. Walk very slowly down the road for five minutes.
11. Stop, inspect minutely, and ask at least six questions about every piece of used chewing gum, dirty tissue and dead insect along the way.
12. Retrace your steps.
13. Scream that you have had as much as you can stand until the neighbours come out and stare at you.
14. Give up and go back into the house.

You are now just about ready to *try* taking a small child for a walk.

Test 7 – Repetition
Repeat everything you say at least five times.

Test 8 – Shopping
Go to the local supermarket. Take with you the nearest thing you can find to a pre-school child (a full-grown goat is excellent). If you intend to have more than one child, take more than one goat. Buy your week's groceries without letting the goat(s) out of your sight. Pay for everything the goat eats or destroys. Until you can easily accomplish this, do not even contemplate having children.

Test 9 – Feeding baby
1. Make a small hole in the side of a melon.
2. Suspend the melon from the ceiling and swing it from side to side.
3. Now get a bowl of soggy cornflakes and attempt to spoon them into the swaying melon by pretending to be an aeroplane.
4. Continue until half the cornflakes are gone.
5. Tip the rest into your lap, making sure that a lot of it falls on the floor.

You are now ready to feed a twelve-month-old child.

Test 10 – Intellectual stimulation
Learn the names of every character from *Barney*, *Teletubbies* and Disney. Watch nothing else on TV for at least five years.

Test 11 – Ruining the furniture
Can you stand the mess children make? To find out, smear peanut butter onto the sofa and jam onto the curtains. Hide a fish behind the stereo and leave it there all summer. Stick your fingers in the flower beds, then wipe them on the clean walls. Cover the stains with crayon. How does that look?

Test 12 – Road-tripping with baby
Make a recording of Barbara Woodhouse shouting, 'Mummy!' repeatedly. Important: no more than a four-second delay between each 'Mummy' and an occasional

crescendo to the level of a supersonic jet is required. Play this CD in your car, everywhere you go, for the next four years. You are now ready to take a long trip with a toddler.

Test 13 – Socialising

Start talking to an adult of your choice. Have someone else continuously tug on your skirt hem/shirtsleeve/elbow while playing the 'Mummy' tape from Test 12 above. You are now ready to have a conversation with an adult while there is a child in the room.

Test 14 – Personal presentation

Put on your finest work attire. Pick a day on which you have an important meeting. Now:
1. Take a cup of cream, and put one cup of lemon juice in it.
2. Stir.
3. Dump half of it on your nice silk shirt. Saturate a towel with the other half of the mixture.
4. Attempt to clean your shirt with the saturated towel.
5. Do NOT change. You have no time.
6. Go directly to work.

Test 15 – Driving baby and sibling

Go for a drive, but first:
1. Find one large tomcat and a pit bull.
2. Borrow a child safety seat and put it in the back seat of your car.
3. Put the pit bull in the front seat of your car.
4. While holding something fragile or delicate, strap the cat into the child seat.
5. For the really adventurous … run some errands, remove and replace the cat at each stop.

You are now ready to have kids.

(Extracted and adapted from various sites on the internet; original source unknown)

CINDERELLA SELLS OUT

'Being a princess isn't all it's cracked up to be.'
> — *Diana, Princess of Wales (1961–1997)*

When you read the part in the book that says I was horrified with the women who had allowed their husbands to buy them cars, did you secretly think that you are happy with, or hoping for, Prince Charming to buy you a car? If so, you may have what is known as the 'Cinderella Complex'.

I found the following information on the Cinderella Complex on www.wikipedia.com (edited):

> *First described by Colette Dowling, who wrote a book on women's unconscious desire to be taken care of by others, based primarily on a fear of being independent. The importance of [the] book is not the theory of independence that she sets forth. The importance of the work can be defined as identifying an aspect of a larger phenomenon as to why women choose to stay in dysfunctional relationships.*

The Cinderella Complex has become a common term in financial circles to describe women who have handed their financial well-being to their husbands. Wikipedia goes on to say:

> *This complex is named after the fairy-tale character Cinderella, popularised by the Disney movie of the same name. It is based on the idea of women that the story portrays, as being beautiful, graceful and polite, but who cannot be strong, independent characters themselves, and who must be rescued by an outside force, usually a man (the Prince).*

I had a friend – let's call her Nancy – who, thinking about it now, had an extreme case of the Cinderella Complex. There were several warning signs:
– Every man she met was weighed up as a potential husband (which naturally had them heading for the hills).

- Other women's men were fair game.
- Although very bright and capable, she never pushed herself to study or to achieve beyond the bare minimum.
- She took no responsibility for her financial affairs and refused to learn the basics of financial planning.
- She was a classic victim, never accepting responsibility for her actions – everything was always someone else's fault.

It was very clear that Nancy was, and probably still is, waiting for Prince Charming to rescue her. She got more and more depressed as time went by and her prince failed to appear. Eventually she was left with no job, massive debt and no man – somewhat like Cinderella before Prince Charming arrived. But this was the end, not the start, of her story. And still she waits.

I recently read an article on the Cinderella Complex at www.ioljobs.co.za. It looked at women who had married their princes and handed over their financial lives to their husbands, only to be faced with 'princes' who subsequently upped and left. Contrary to popular belief, women – even if their husbands leave them for another woman – don't always get a house, a car and an income when their marriages end. And, with more than 50 per cent of marriages ending in divorce these days, it is a precarious existence Cinderella has created for herself and her children (if she has any).

Suze Orman, the world-famous American financial advisor – voted by *Time* magazine as one of the most influential people in the world – has written many books, six of which are bestsellers, on the subject of finance for women. You owe it to yourself to buy at least one of her books to get some insight into why you need to – and how you can – become financially independent. Take responsibility for providing for yourself and your children, and *then* you can live happily ever after.

Chapter **4**

RUNG 1:
LUST, LOVE AND MENTORS

HOW FAR IS IT TO THE TOP?

> 'Climbing to the top demands strength, whether it is to the top of
> Mount Everest or to the top of your career.'
> — *Dr APJ Abdul Kalam (President of India; 1931–?)*

So we've tackled the sticky subjects of being divas or doormats, of being victims
or changing outlooks, of stereotypes and attitudes, and of kids vs careers. We
are now ready to take a look at what you need to do to climb the first rung of the
corporate ladder.

Before you haul out your climbing Choos, how big is the ladder you want to
ascend? Do you want to go all the way to the top of a long ladder – as in being
Mr or Ms Big of a large corporation – or would you be happy in the middle of
that ladder, which means you rise to middle management? Perhaps you want to
be at the top of a shorter ladder, as in the big boss of a smaller company, or maybe
your own company?

Climbing the ladder does not literally have to mean becoming the boss. It can also
mean climbing to the very top of your profession – being the top salesperson, the
best strategist or a phenomenal teacher. I would rather be an exceptional salesperson
than the big boss any day – that way I would also get to earn more than Mr Big!

Let me explain it another way: imagine that you are a brilliant gymnast who loves the physicality of the sport. Climbing the gymnastic ladder, in this sense, would mean becoming the best gymnast in your country, or in the world. It does not necessarily mean that you want to become a national coach or head of gymnastics for the Olympics committee. So, when I talk about climbing the ladder, remember to bear this in mind.

Whatever you choose is just fine – the rules of the game remain more or less the same. If you're unsure as to how far you want to go, but you know that you want to go *up*, that's fine too. We will also take a look at what will be expected of you at the top, but for now, let's get you started on that ladder.

There are so many choices the women of today need to make – from the small ones, like what to wear and which diet to follow, to the major ones, such as what career path to take, who to marry, kids vs career, and so on. No matter what your choices, you need to be sure that these are the right ones for *you*. Don't let your parents, friends, husband or whoever make these choices for you, or push you in a direction with which you are not comfortable – you are the one who has to live with the consequences of any decisions. This is an important part of not selling your soul.

If you are reading this book, you are probably living in the 'free world' – a world where women are blessed with the freedom to make their own choices. By embracing this freedom, we can repay our debt to the pioneering women who sacrificed so much to give us a world in which we get to control our own destinies. In leading by example, we also help pave the way for those women who are still treated as lesser forms of life.

Time magazine of 24 March 2008 featured an article entitled '10 Ideas that Are Changing the World'. Idea #9, written by Vivienne Walt, is 'Women's Work. Tapping the female entrepreneurial spirit can pay big dividends'. Here is an extract from the article:

Economists have long believed that the least productive societies are those in which women are denied opportunities to join the workforce. In underdeveloped countries, women typically go without the most basic tools needed to earn a living: education, training and access to capital. Yet there is abundant evidence linking economic progress with empowered women.

The article goes on to say how much funding is being made available for the development of women:

> *The World Bank began funding management training for women in Tanzania and Uganda. This month investment bank Goldman Sachs announced it would spend $100 million over the next five years on business education for 10,000 women entrepreneurs in Asia, Africa and the Middle East.*

Are we in the right place at the right time, or what?

HOT, SIZZLING PASSION

> 'Without passion, you don't have energy; without energy, you have nothing.' – *Donald Trump (American entrepreneur; 1946–?)*

Now that we're all fired up, let's put our beautifully shod feet on the first rung of the corporate ladder. And that rung is called 'personal investment and development'. 'No!' I hear you yelling. 'I want to take huge big leaps up the ladder. I'm done with studying. I'll pick it up as I go along!' You *can* just pick it up as you go – in fact, you *have* to pick it up as you go – but if you want to rise to the top of your ladder, you need to be prepared to invest a lot more in yourself than merely 'picking it up'.

Imagine you are going on a date with a really hot man. He's invited you to a show and dinner for the following week. Fifty bucks says you spend a *lot* of time thinking about what you'll wear, what you'll talk about and how far you'll let things go. You may even treat yourself to a new outfit. The planning is part of the thrill, and it is the investment you make from your side to ensure that the date lives up to your expectations. Try to view investing in your career in the same way. It can – and should – be fun.

Gary Player *(South African world-class golfer; 1935– ?)* is attributed with saying, 'The harder I practise, the luckier I get.' The same will apply to your career. Every successful businesswoman to whom I have ever spoken has always been at pains to point out that she worked very hard, made many sacrifices, and had to spend a lot of time learning and reading, asking questions and researching, in order to get to the top. Joan Joffe *(South African Businesswoman of the Year in 1987)* is a case in point. I had the honour of working for Joan in the late 1980s, and I have yet to see anyone work harder than her.

There is the occasional woman I hear about who has allegedly been 'lucky'. Have another look at Gary Player's quote. I personally have never met a successful businesswoman who thinks her rise to the top of her profession has been a fairy tale. You owe it to yourself to invest in yourself.

What does 'personal investment and development' actually mean? Well, it's about the way you look, the words you use, the people you know, the depth of your knowledge, the time and preparation you invest in projects that may or may not come off, the long hours, the sacrifices, etc. It doesn't exactly sound like a walk in the park, does it? But imagine that this is what's required of you for your dream wedding. You would be happy to make these investments. Why not in your career?

The secret to making your career as interesting and exciting as your wedding is one simple little word: *passion*. If you are not passionate about getting ahead, you are unlikely to be willing to make the sacrifices needed to become the Work Diva of your dreams. If you are hoping it will 'just happen', this is the same as waiting for Prince Charming to come along on his white horse and whip you off to happily-ever-after land. If you don't have the passion, girl, divadom just isn't gonna happen for you.

On the subject of passion, did you know that when a man died, the ancient Greeks asked only one thing about his life: Did he have passion? Where did I learn this? From the movie *Serendipity*, with the delectable John Cusack. You can learn a lot from the movies, but be sure to verify the information (I'm not sure about this Greek theory thing, but it sounds right, doesn't it?).

How has passion affected my career? I did not have a great time at school. Sure, I enjoyed my girlfriends and going to parties and being in love with the boys and all that, but I hated the restrictions imposed on me in the school environment, much of it by teachers I didn't respect. Anyhow, in the middle of my second-last year of high school, the deputy headmistress told me that I would be expelled if I didn't move schools (sorry, Dad, if you didn't know this). I was coincidentally moved to a boarding school at that time, and although it was the happiest period of my school life, I still did not excel. The headmistress of the boarding school is rumoured to have said that she expected me to end up in jail within two years of my leaving school.

The problem was I had no passion for school, other than in the classes of the teachers who made their subjects interesting – English and Geography. Strange, that. On leaving school, there was no money for university (and girls, in those days, seldom got offered bursaries), so my father decided that I should become an air hostess in order for me to see the world. Over my dead body was I going to become an air hostess, so I took the first job I could find – a teller at a building society. Perhaps not the most auspicious start, I'm sure you'll agree, but I worked hard and could serve twice as many people as any of the other girls from my intake (albeit without any finesse at all). Why did I work hard in a job well beneath my capabilities? Simple: I got a kick out of the business environment.

My next job – I was only nineteen – was as a recruitment consultant. I knew bugger-all about anything, so how they could have hired me, heaven only knows. I was their top performer for the first six months, but I lost interest and quit before I could be fired. My next position was as a personnel officer, then I became a human resources manager, and then a human resources director. I subsequently started my own business, eventually returning to the business world as an executive director of strategy for a listed company (if you don't know what a listed company is, find out pronto). I became, if my boss was to be believed, the second-highest-paid woman on the African continent.

Why am I telling you all of this? Well, two of the reasons I got ahead were that I worked hard and I studied while I was working. But, most importantly, I had, and still have, a passion for the business environment and learning everything I could about business. Even though some of my jobs were pretty modest, I still got a thrill out of being the best I could in the big bad world of business.

Are you prepared to work hard and ready to have some fun?

LEARNING TO LOVE LEARNING

> 'Live as if you're going to die tomorrow, learn as if you're going to live
> forever.'   – *Chinese proverb, also attributed to*
> *Mohandas Gandhi (Indian philosopher; 1869–1948)*

There are people in this world who are afraid to admit that there is stuff they don't know. They think they will look stupid if they admit to not being an expert on all subjects known to mankind. I call these people 'I-Specialists'. 'I' this, 'I' that. I (watch out, Kim!) suspect that they are trying to disguise how little they know by talking about themselves. Continually. Ask them a question where it would normally be impossible to talk about oneself and, hey presto, you get an 'I' answer (try this with the I-Specialists you know – it's a great game!). An integral part of climbing the Work Diva ladder is knowing what you don't know – and not being too proud to learn.

I mentioned in the previous chapter that I studied while I was working because there was no money for a university education. One of the greatest influences on my business life has been Nic Frangos (you will probably know him as golf legend Ernie Els's manager during the height of Ernie's career). Nic is a successful and influential businessman and was my mentor for most of the 1980s. Nic wanted me to study further. He said that many of the careers I might want to pursue would be closed to me because I did not have a degree. He explained that a degree would be the key to opening lots of doors.

My degree took me four years (ever the underperforming student), but, finally, I held it in my grubby little paws. Has it made a whole lot of difference to me as a person? Not really. But let me tell you, that degree changed the way people saw me and *was* the key to opening doors that would otherwise have been closed. I found working (Nic was a very demanding employer) *and* trying to have a social life *and* studying almost impossible at times, but it is probably the investment that has paid back the most in terms of personal dividends.

Nic also taught me about Fritz, the guy who didn't always 'get it'. Fritz was the very talented, but not necessarily smartest, player in an American football team coached by the great Vince Lombardi. When Fritz didn't understand something, which was pretty often, Lombardi would patiently explain whatever it was that Fritz needed to know. Nic encouraged me, and the other members of his executive team, to play 'Fritz' – if I didn't know what someone was talking about in management meetings (or anywhere else, for that matter), I should raise my hand and say, 'I'm Fritz. Please explain what you just said (or what you mean) to me.'

In this way, I would always know what was going on. I was only in my early twenties at the time, so there was a *lot* I didn't know. Nic said that I was only stupid if I didn't ask questions or challenge something with which I didn't agree. To this day, I still ask questions when I don't know what people are talking about. And that is still a lot of the time!

How does this impact you, the aspiring Work Diva? In the immortal words of Bono *(Irish singer; 1960–?)*, 'The less you know, the more you believe.' Empower yourself with knowledge. Make Google your best friend. It may mean that you need to study further. It will definitely mean that you will have to learn a lot (and ask millions of questions) as you climb the ladder, but it is the one thing that nobody can take away from you. You can lose your possessions or your job or your loved ones, but your knowledge will always belong to you.

Still need more encouragement? Think about it like this: If you were the chief executive officer (CEO) or managing director of a large organisation and were looking to hire someone for a senior position, would you employ the person who had invested in themselves in terms of further study, courses, and expanding their knowledge and experience base, or the person who had not made these investments? You know the answer.

LEARNING TO INVEST

'If a man empties his purse into his head, no man can take it away from him. An investment in knowledge always pays the best interest.'
– *Benjamin Franklin (one of the founding fathers*
of the USA; 1706–1790)

To become the Work Diva that everyone wants to hire, there is no better investment you can make in your career than investing in yourself. Earlier I defined 'personal investment and development' as the way you look, the words you use, the people you know, the depth of your knowledge, the time and preparation you invest in projects, etc. The subject of investment is so important, it deserves a lot more attention.

Let's talk about you. When you stand up to be counted, stripped and alone, what will people see? Have you made the most of yourself? Are you investing in your own shares? Do you push yourself to be the best you can be? Are you a diva of substance? Have you earned the respect of those around you?

The investment you need to make in yourself operates on several levels. Let's use Maslow's Hierarchy of Needs to explain the different levels. Abraham Maslow *(American psychologist; 1908–1970)* is considered to be the father of humanistic psychology (which basically means he was the first psychologist to emphasise the difference between humans and other species, based on the human need for personal development and psychological growth).

The simplest explanation of Maslow's Hierarchy of Needs is the following (with a little help from www.wikipedia.com): Maslow saw human beings' needs arranged like a ladder:

- The most basic needs, at the bottom, were survival (Level 1): air, water, food, shelter, sex.
- Then came the safety needs (Level 2): a sense of security through property, employment, family, morality.
- These were followed by a sense of belonging or social needs (Level 3): love, acceptance, intimacy, friends.
- Second from the top were needs of esteem (Level 4): self-esteem, confidence, achievement, respect of and by others.
- At the top came the self-actualising needs (Level 5): personal growth and fulfilment, a sense of purpose and meaning, spontaneity, creativity, lack of prejudice, problem-solving.

Read up on this – it really is interesting. Maslow's Hierarchy expressed as a diagram looks like this:

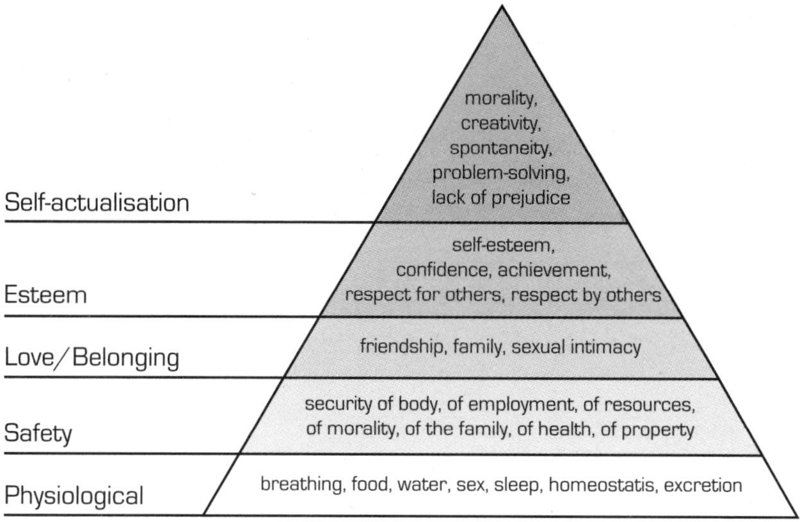
Self-actualisation
morality,
creativity,
spontaneity,
problem-solving,
lack of prejudice
Esteem
self-esteem,
confidence, achievement,
respect for others, respect by others
Love/Belonging
friendship, family, sexual intimacy
Safety
security of body, of employment, of resources,
of morality, of the family, of health, of property
Physiological
breathing, food, water, sex, sleep, homeostatis, excretion

(Extracted from www.wikipedia.com)

Let's start at the bottom of the hierarchy – Level 1, as I've called it. If your basic needs aren't met – you have no air, food or shelter, for example – you never rise above that level. At Level 2, you have a physical need to be part of a group, have a roof over your head, and so on. Level 3 is the emotional need for friends and family – a sense of belonging. You've already reached this level, so on to Level 4. If you're reading this book, I can safely assume that you are aware of your need for self-esteem and respect! Next comes Level 5 – and this is where we have to stretch ourselves to self-actualise. What is self-actualisation? It's the need for personal growth and development, for having a sense of purpose and meaning in our lives.

To be a self-actualised person, you must *need* personal growth. This is, after all, the essence of Maslow's Hierarchy of *Needs*. Feeding this need for growth, however, leads to learning, and learning is a lifelong love affair. Once you start learning, you realise how little you know, and so you learn, to fill the gap; and the more you know, the more you realise what you don't know, so you learn some more. You get addicted to learning, and it's a need you can never fully satisfy. It's like a lover of whom you never tire. It's a drug.

The good news about this need for love and drugs in the form of personal growth and development is that it will get you to the top, as opposed to just high. And it will keep you there, rather than dumping you in the gutter like other addictions.

If we take Level 5 from Maslow's Hierarchy and split it into five steps, we can create our very own 'Diva Investment Needs Hierarchy', which looks like this:

1. Step A: physical appearance and impressions – making the most of what I have.
2. Step B: attitude – airs, graces and being the best me that I can be.
3. Step C: alignment with others – mentors for learning, sisters for support.
4. Step D: respect – both earned and given.
5. Step E: growth and purpose – links back to and supports each of the other levels and is achieved through a love of learning.

Investing in yourself is not selfish. It is essential for your very survival, or so says Abraham Maslow. If you are not prepared to invest in yourself, how can you expect anyone else to be prepared to invest in you?

WHERE SHALL I GO? WHAT SHALL I DO?

> 'Share your knowledge. It's a way to achieve immortality.'
> – *The Dalai Lama (Tibetan spiritual leader; 1935–?)*

Picking up on our Diva Investment Needs Hierarchy, we are going to leap ahead to Step C (we'll come back to A and B in a moment). You may have noticed that earlier I mentioned the names of two influential people for whom I have worked. No, I am not shamelessly dropping names – I mentioned them for a reason. They are amongst the most influential people in my career – my mentors. How did they become my mentors? Was it a formal arrangement? Did they even know they were my mentors?

I've always been greedy when it comes to knowledge. Knowledge is not only about learning – it's about your interest in the world, the people of the planet, the goings-on around you. If you have a passion for gossip, you're on the right path.

A big word of caution on gossip, though – how you use the gossip to which you are privy is very important. If it's simply information because you're interested in people, we're on the same page, but if it's to hurt another person or hold power over them in some way, it's not the same thing at all. Using gossip to damage someone else will ultimately burn you. We'll gossip about gossip later.

Being this knowledge gannet, I've constantly wanted answers – and who better to ask than the boss? Nic Frangos was not my first mentor. When I look back at all my bosses and superiors, I probably started developing mentors as a teller at the building society. I used to observe Maria, the most senior of the tellers; I asked my supervisor for guidance and fiddled with the computer at every available opportunity. This is how I stumbled upon mentoring. I would love to say that finding mentors was some clever strategy on my part, but the reality is that it just sort of evolved – more ass than class.

Most people are willing to share their knowledge. In fact, most people enjoy the opportunity to show you how much they know. All you have to do is ask. Ask questions of everyone around you. Ask for input from the people above you and below you in the company's hierarchy. Do yourself a favour, though, and *listen to the answers.* You don't have to blindly accept the information you are given – apply your intelligence to their answers – but have the courtesy to listen to what they say. In this way you will learn the most, the quickest.

Don't be coy about setting out to find yourself a mentor. Find someone you admire and respect and ask them if they would be prepared to guide you. Take the time to establish *their* expectations from the interactions. I didn't ask Joan Joffe or Nic Frangos to mentor me – I probably didn't have enough confidence at the time to be that bold – but an informal relationship evolved. Now, with hindsight, I wish the arrangement had been more formal, but that would have been up to me to initiate.

I was approached recently by a lovely, intelligent young woman who was intrepid enough to ask me if I was prepared to be her mentor. I had not met her before, but agreed to have a session with her. During our conversation I explained that I wanted two things from her side – she must always be on time, and she needed to attend my entry-level course on deal-making (at no cost). It was very important to me that we were on the same page. For our first meeting, she was half an hour late. She also never took me up on the offer of attending the course. So, as much as we liked each other, a mentor relationship would not work. We chose friendship instead. Respecting your mentor's time and expectations is an integral part of the relationship, so before you ask someone to mentor you, be sure you are prepared to make the investment from your side.

Choosing and approaching a potential mentor is a tricky matter. A mentor is the work equivalent of a fairy godmother, but you still have to do all the work yourself. Their role is to guide you, not rescue you. Ideally your mentor should be someone:

– for whom you already work (as you will then have ready access to the person), or
– in a senior position to you, whose respect you are in the process of earning (so they'll be prepared to invest the time from their side), or
– not necessarily in your company, but for whom you have a high regard.

Be aware that not all the guidance you get will be what you want to hear – Joan Joffe once encouraged me to abandon my favourite pair of white shoes (I cringe with horror at the thought of them now) – but make the assumption that your mentor will give you the guidance you need at that time. Also, remember that the person you are asking to be your mentor is probably very busy, so a lot of the time you need to spend with them will be after hours and will require extra effort on your part. Hard work, here you come!

Why not ask a friend or lover or family member, or any other individual with whom you have a personal relationship, to mentor you? Be *very* careful about doing this, as any unfavourable or critical feedback they give you may harm your relationship. It is far easier to hear the negative stuff from someone who is an outsider, or with whom you have a professional relationship. My advice? Avoid a personal-relationship mentor at all costs, as it can lead to unnecessary tension between the two of you.

If you find that lovers, friends and family give you career advice – solicited or not – use your judgement as to whether you will act on their advice. You are a Work Diva in the making – you need to make up your own mind about what will be good or bad for your career.

How many mentors should you have? The more the merrier, but with each mentor, you will be expected to put in extra effort (have another look at what Gary Player said about hard work). Although I am in the position where I can now share my knowledge with others, I personally still look for mentors.

Kanya King, MBE, and founder of the MOBO (Music of Black Origin) Awards, had this to say about mentors at a recent international conference: 'I'm always looking for mentors and have always had great people around who have given me fantastic advice; nobody can do it on their own.'

What is the difference between a mentor and a coach? As I see it, a mentor is interested in the personal growth and development of the individual with whom he or she has a mentoring relationship, whereas a coach wants to maximise the performance of the individual in a specific area. The mentor is thus a more generic support system, while the coach fixes specific areas. For example, as his manager, Nic Frangos mentored Ernie Els, whereas David Leadbetter was Ernie's professional coach. Make sense? If not, there is a lot of information on the internet detailing the differences between the two.

The vast majority of my mentors have been a good influence on me, although some have taught me what *not* to do, more than what to do! Without exception, they cared deeply about helping me and shared their knowledge liberally. I believe this generosity stemmed from the fact that I was genuinely eager to learn. A quick word of thanks to some of the fantastic mentors in my life: Terry Dearling, who treated me like an equal; Joan Joffe, who showed me the power that lies in behaving like a lady; Patrick Evans, who guided and misled me in equal proportions; Bob Strain, for teaching me that business can be fun; Dr Karen Toombs, for making me confront my demons; Nick Speare, who taught me how to *really* sell; Gary Harlow, who taught me about corporate finance and the importance of passion in deal-making; and especially Nic Frangos, who encouraged the extremely raw material with which he was working to be entrepreneurial, to expect a lot from herself and always to have a ten-year plan.

In the film *Gone With the Wind*, Scarlett O'Hara says, 'Where shall I go? What shall I do?' Well, dear Scarlett, the answer is, 'Go find yourself a mentor, girl.'

Chapter 5

RUNG 2:
THE WORK DIVA'S SENSE OF STYLE

PIGEONHOLES FOR PEOPLE

'Behaviour is a mirror in which every one displays his image.'
– *Johann Wolfgang von Goethe (German writer; 1749–1832)*

Now that you have got past the first rung of your ladder – a passion for business, a lifelong commitment to learning and finding suitable mentors – you need to make sense of the people in your work environment. The easiest way to do this is to 'classify' them according to their style of behaviour. 'That's putting people in boxes,' I hear you object. You may be right, so skip this section if it makes you uncomfortable, but it is also the simplest way to understand what is sometimes pretty baffling conduct on the part of the people with whom you work.

For many years, psychologists and researchers have been using a general classification system to define behaviour. Some people call it personality profiles, but the more learned people (and you want to be one of those, right?) refer to it as behavioural analysis. The most common tool, still used today, is the DiSC (Dominance, influencing, Steadiness and Conscientiousness) behavioural model developed in the 1920s by American psychologist Dr William Moulton Marston. The fact that so many people have copied or modified the original work of Dr Marston suggests that there must be merit in his classification system. Somewhere along your climb up the corporate ladder, you will be required to take a 'personality test'. The chances are pretty good that the origins of that test will be in the DiSC model.

If you have already been exposed to personality types, social styles or a similar profiling-type course, you will know that there are two axes along which a person's behaviour is generally measured. Dr Marston defined the first axis (or line) as 'assert vs yield'. This axis is also referred to as 'A type vs B type', or 'competitive vs cooperative', or 'tense vs easy-going', or even 'dominant vs passive'. I tend to describe this axis as 'aggressive vs agreeable'.

The second axis identified by Dr Marston is the 'antagonised by vs allied with' range. It is also known as the 'extrovert vs introvert', 'impulsive vs controlled', 'warm vs cool' or 'spontaneous vs self-controlled' axis. I prefer to use the words 'sceptical vs receptive' to describe this axis.

When plotted as one vertical axis and one horizontal axis, the two axes cross each other, forming four quadrants. In a diagram, they would appear as follows:

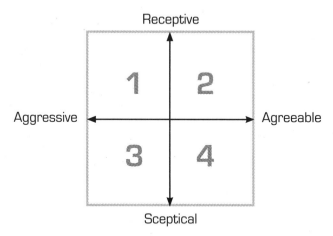

Each of the four quadrants is then given a name, usually a word that describes the behaviour defined by that quadrant. For example, a person falling into quadrant 1 (i.e. the Receptive/Aggressive quadrant) is commonly referred to as an 'Expressive'

or similar. A person in quadrant 2 (Receptive/Agreeable) is often called an 'Amiable'. Collectively, the Expressives and Amiables are the 'warm' people. The quadrant 3 Aggressive/Sceptical person is known as a 'Driver', and the Agreeable/Sceptical individual of quadrant 4 an 'Analytical'. These are the 'cool' people. Grouping the Expressives and Drivers together will give you the 'A-type' personality, whereas the Amiables and Analyticals are 'B type'. If you don't like these names or words, feel free to choose your own!

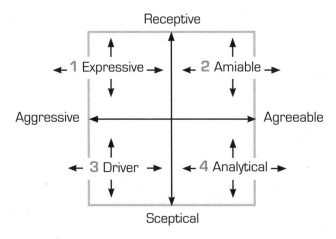

It is important to appreciate that the purpose of these classifications is not really to pigeonhole people as such, but to help us understand their social behaviour. There is obviously a lot more theory behind this, but by recognising whether a person is, firstly, Receptive or Sceptical, and, secondly, Aggressive or Agreeable, we get an insight into their personality that enables us to get along better with those we do not like. It also helps us to understand why we are drawn to other people. This is important in the workplace.

Having a tool like this to use is a blast. When you meet someone, you can quickly guess into which block they would fit – and the vast majority of the time you would be right! Once you've done your 'assessment', you need to think about how you will interact with that person. Here is a brief description of each behavioural style, with an outline of how to engage with that particular style in a business-meeting environment – and what to watch for in your own style (because, by now, you've probably figured out in which quadrant you fit). Each style does, of course, have its very own 'good' and 'bad' list! In the next chapter we'll have a closer look at these behaviours and the women in the office.

1. Expressives

The party girls and drama queens of the behavioural styles. They are confident, sociable, enthusiastic, energetic, impulsive, creative, charming, persuasive, supportive, flighty, manipulative, competitive. They lack detail, are undisciplined and overreactive.

When dealing with Expressives – who are Receptive yet Aggressive – you need to keep the meeting light in tone to avoid confrontation and ensure that any presentation or proposal you make is not mired in detail. Expressives are likely to show an immediate, usually positive, reaction to your proposal, but afterwards you may battle to pin them down. If you push them too hard, they can get pretty tense with you. They are decisive, but you will need to agree to an action plan. If *you* are the Expressive, people will gravitate towards you because you are charismatic and engaging, but because of your love for showman-like antics, others may not take you seriously. Also, watch that ego!

2. Amiables

Miss Congeniality herself and the Queen of Hearts. Amiables are friendly, kind, people-orientated, sympathetic, considerate, willing, supportive, dependable, respectful, conflict-averse, relaxed, indecisive, defensive, easily intimidated.

The Amiables, falling into the Receptive/Agreeable quadrant, are the 'nice guys' of the world. Being nice guys, they do not want to disappoint you and may send you the wrong signals about your presentation or proposal. Be aware that they are also nice to everyone else, so where you might think you have an ally, they may be on *everyone's* side, not just yours. Amiables can be dismissed by others as indecisive or ineffective. If you are an Amiable, people will love you but leave you, because they perceive you as not being able to make decisions. A bit more directness, albeit in your own kind manner, will go a long way!

3. Drivers

The decision-makers and the bitches. Drivers are direct, independent, organised, determined, focused, pragmatic, honest, results-orientated, demanding, critical, pushy, harsh, aggressive, competitive.

If you are going into a meeting with someone who is Aggressive and Sceptical, you will be dealing with a Driver. You know that they will be cynical about what you are saying, and because they are aggressive by nature, conflict or confrontation can be easily sparked. You may want to modify your approach with Drivers to that of a more fact-based, non-confrontational style, as you do not want to increase the tension level of the meeting. On the upside, Drivers are decisive. If *your* style is that of a Driver, you need to pay attention to the niceties of a meeting and guard against being perceived as arrogant. I am a Driver, so I need to be careful of being seen as humourless and rude.

4. Analyticals

The diplomats and Little Miss Detail. Analyticals are respectful, tactful, listeners, obedient, persistent, industrious, logical, systematic, orderly, deliberate, organised, detailed, stubborn, cautious, tedious, anal.

As Agreeable/Sceptical, Analyticals are not obviously decisive and will want a lot of detail from you before they make a decision. Be sure to include the facts and figures when dealing with Analyticals. They will consider all facets of your proposal and still may hesitate to give you a decision. Remember, they are Agreeable and don't want to disappoint you, so they may avoid giving you an answer rather than giving you a negative one. If you are Analytical, you like to feel personally comfortable with the people you deal with, but, like the Amiable, you need to communicate bad news openly. Watch out for an interesting trait you have: stubbornness!

The worst person to interact with an Analytical is an Expressive, because an Expressive is the polar opposite of an Analytical. By the way, the Driver and the Amiable are opposites too.

If you are thinking, 'But there's more to me than just one style – I have a little of all of them in me,' you would be right! When we relax or are under pressure, our behaviour can and does change. A Driver may become more Amiable or Expressive, an Analytical more Expressive, and so on – but that requires another whole level of analysis. Suffice to say that understanding a person's general social behavioural style will go a long way in helping you to shape and manage the relationships you build with other people.

What is very important to remember, though, is that *you are who you are.* In analysing these behavioural styles, I am not advocating that you change your inherent character – you need to be true to yourself – but I am suggesting that if you are prepared to modify your *behaviour*, you will be arming yourself with a very powerful tool when it comes to dealing with other people and getting what you want.

I wonder if there is any connection between the behavioural styles and the star signs? I suspect there might be!

(First published in *Succeed* magazine in July 2006, copyright Kim Meredith)

THE EIGHT DIVAS YOU MEET AT WORK

> 'I'm tough, I'm ambitious, and I know exactly what I want. If that makes me a bitch, okay.'   *– Madonna (American singer, songwriter and actress; 1958–?)*

One of the joys of the workplace is that it's like going shopping for shoes and finding an amazing store where they have absolutely every style for which you could possibly wish. Sure, there'll be a few pairs you can't stand and there'll be a lot towards which you are indifferent, but there will also be some gorgeous gems that you just know will fit like a glove – or is that a glass slipper? See your colleagues as shoes and you'll never again view them in the same light!

We've spoken about the four behavioural styles into which people fit and I promised we'd look at the women in the office in more detail, but before we do that, let's mention men very briefly. In a nutshell, we are not going to be analysing the men, as this is the *Work Diva's* guide – *for* Work Divas and *about* Work Divas. Now, back to the girls and some light relief. Try to figure out into which of the eight categories listed below you fall, and then check that category against the behavioural styles in the previous section – you will see that all the dots connect.

1. The party girl

You are the life and soul of the party. People fight over you accepting *their* invitation. You laugh, you joke, you drink too much tequila and then take off your clothes. The next morning people are embarrassed for you, although you are not embarrassed for yourself. Everyone wants to be your friend because you get invited everywhere. You take pride in how you look and love telling people what to do with their lives. You are your own legend.

In the workplace you are extremely popular, especially with the men, but your bosses don't seem to take you terribly seriously. If your boss, partner or friend tells you to tone down your behaviour, you think it's best to ignore them – you are popular for a reason, so they must be wrong! Lindsay Lohan is your secret diva.

2. The drama queen

You are larger than life and, because of this, people are drawn to you. You know everything about everyone and enjoy being included in the personal lives of others. Although you are inclined to gossip, you know which secrets to keep. If anyone needs someone to fight their cause, they run to you. You are the original 'champion of the underdog'. You like bling drinks that nobody knows how to make, champagne and limousines. When you go to a party, you make a grand entrance. Men are intimidated by you but can't help being drawn to you.

At work you have a faithful band of followers who would be prepared to go to war for you. One problem: the bosses don't want to promote you, as they think you like making a fuss just for the sake of it. The diva you think has it all is Jennifer Lopez.

3. Miss Congeniality

Men and women alike adore you. You were always one of the most popular people in your school, and it is the same in the workplace. You genuinely care about everyone and there are very few people you dislike. You have a ready smile on your face and know of a million ways in which to cheer people up. When someone is feeling down, they find themselves wandering into your office for a coffee. Your drink of choice is whatever anyone else is having.

You have trouble deciding which invitations to accept, which men to date, which jobs to accept – in fact, you have problems with decisions, period. You just don't want to hurt anyone's feelings by making choices. The bosses have noticed your tendency to dither and, while they would love to promote you, they worry about your need to be liked. Your inner diva is Sandra Bullock.

4. The Queen of Hearts

If ever anyone needs a date for a dinner or party or a wedding, they dash to see you. You know everyone and generously share your huge social network. You organise parties, where you drink very little – maybe a glass of wine – just so people can meet, and you never expect a return invitation. You measure your wealth by the number of people you know and your success by your matchmaking. People need your opinion on all sorts of romantic subjects, but you see your role as helping them to feel good about all their options. You are surprised that you don't hold a more senior position, given your networking skills, but your bosses find your need to have devoted subjects rather disturbing. You consider Julia Roberts to be a wonderful diva, although Jennifer Aniston is probably the most self-sacrificing diva – and what about Meg Ryan?

5. The decision-maker

People respect you because you make decisions. You would rather make *any* decision than sit on the fence. You know what you want and you go for it. People want to be in your team because they know you will win, even if they are a little scared of you. Scared is not all bad. You have an uncanny ability to defend your decisions, as you are able to show why they were the right ones to make, even if things turned out wrong. People know that when you say you'll be at a function, you'll be there. You'll order a decent single malt, for sure. In the workplace, your bosses have told you to think more before you act, but you know what you know and know that this will get you ahead. Demi Moore *is* the ultimate diva.

6. The bitch

It is not your intention to be a bitch, but people are *so* oversensitive. Why can't they just accept that if you have stuff to do and they get in the way, they'll get burnt? It's not personal. You are fully behind the woman, whoever she was, who coined the phrase, 'You say I'm a bitch like it's a bad thing.' There's a difference between being *perceived* as a bitch, which is the case with you, and actually *being* a bitch. You don't gossip or make catty comments – so how can you be a bitch? People respect you because you don't gossip, for heaven's sake! You know the assholes at the top of the organisation don't like you, but that's because you are a threat to them. Being driven is not easy – just ask Madonna. She's a diva with whom you can definitely identify.

7. The diplomat

You are known as the most tactful person in the company. You have an uncanny ability to say the right thing at the right time. People know that you think about what you are going to say, so, when you say it, they listen to you. You just wish you could command a bit more of their attention instead of always being the listener. You're a popular member of the team because you always make a big effort to ensure that everything is done properly and on time. People appreciate that about you. Your boss has told you that you will go far in the company if you can be more assertive, but you battle to see how you can be assertive and diplomatic at the same time – and being diplomatic is who you are. After giving it much thought, the diva you admire the most is Condoleezza Rice.

8. Little Miss Detail

You were often the teacher's pet, but that was because you worked the hardest in the class, not because you sucked up. You are proud of your attention to detail and believe it has served you well. Although it hurts your feelings when people call you anally retentive and stubborn, you know that any job worth doing is worth doing well. It is this very attitude that gets you included in big projects in the office. Your bosses often praise your work, but they have also told you to lighten up a bit. How can you lighten up when you take your work seriously? Maybe they'll realise that it is better that you are the way you are. You really admire Margaret in the *Dennis the Menace* cartoon.

Which of these eight pairs of shoes fits you the best? Is there one that really doesn't fit? Do you see a little of yourself in most of the divas described here, but some more than others? The eight Work Divas I've described are simply an exaggerated way of bringing the four behavioural styles to life. See how many other divas you can invent. It's quite easy – just take the extremes of your own 'good' and 'bad' lists and *voila*!

A CHEAP IMITATION OR THE REAL DEAL?

> 'What is your name, boy? And don't lie to me, because you live here,
> and I'll find out who you are.'   – *Bill Cosby,*
>   *from his stand-up comedy (American comedian; 1937–?)*

Before we move off the second rung of the Work Diva's ladder, let's take a less frivolous look at the real you and the impact you have on the people around you, especially in business.

What reveals the *authentic* you? Is it your behaviour (which exposes your underlying character, which, in turn, overlays your attitudes and values)? Is it the words you choose to use? Maybe it's the way you dress or the people with whom you associate? Could it be your choice of partner, or where you live, or the car you drive? What about the position you hold or where you studied, the pets you do or don't have, where you holiday? Of all these factors, there are two that represent the real you – your behaviour and your words. You can dress like a lady, but if you behave like a tramp, people see the tramp. Can you control your behaviour and language? I believe you can. This means you can also control the way you impact the lives of the people with whom you work (and live, by the way).

Imagine your life is a movie and you have chosen to star in the role of 'you'. As a woman, it is very difficult to play the part of a man; if you're an adult, it is hard to be a child, and so on. In preparing for the part of 'you', you need to consider a whole host of elements – the way you will look, how you'll behave, your script, etc. You will win the Oscar only if your performance is authentic and believable. Real life imitates art in this way. In playing 'you', you're aware of the script and actions required of you, but your unconscious words and behaviour will always reflect the real you. The audience watching your performance can see the role you are playing, but they also see the real you underneath this role. If you want to change the underlying you in any way – maybe you need to make a few adjustments to win the Oscar – you need to start by being more aware of your behaviour and rehearsing your words.

Let's start with behaviour. We have had a look at the four behavioural styles, and you have presumably identified with the one that best describes your behaviour (if you haven't done the exercise yet, now's a good time to do it). Recognise what is 'good' and 'bad' in your style. If you want a deeper understanding of this, do a little research on the internet or buy a book (an excellent one is *Personality Plus: How to Understand Others by Understanding Yourself More* by Florence Littauer). Next, identify the 'good' you want to emphasise and decide which 'bads' you want to let go. Consciously start working on the changes you want or need to make and trust that your superconscious will lend a helping hand. This is the essence of how your 'good' and 'bad' lists work.

I mentioned earlier that I'm a Driver. Heaven only knows how I ended up in human resources! Anyhow, I realised that when I started lecturing, I needed to be more of a showman to make an impact (is there anything more dreadful than a rude lecturer?). Richard Rowland, with whom I have had the pleasure of working all over the globe, and who is arguably one of the best lecturers on the planet, calls the lecturer showmen 'entertrainers'. The first one I ever saw was Tom Peters, in one of his videos – and it was amazing. To become an 'entertrainer' meant that I would have to seriously modify my behaviour. It was difficult, I can tell you, for a self-controlled person like me to become an extrovert. I went on courses and practised, and practised some more. Now when I ask people what they believe my behavioural style to be, they say Expressive. I think I've won my Oscar.

So, now you know the secrets for getting beyond the second rung of the corporate ladder without laddering your stockings. Go get that Oscar, girl!

IS IT YOU OR IS IT ME?

'When you blame others, you give up your power to change.'
— *Dr Robert Anthony (American behavioural psychologist,
author and motivator)*

From time to time (and it should *only* be from time to time) you will meet someone with whom you have a spectacular personality clash. Is it you, or is it them? If you clash with lots of people, spot the pattern, sunshine.

Personality clashes, like attitude, can be managed. Here's a wonderful story to illustrate how changing your attitude can impact those around you.

Slow poison

A long time ago in China, a girl named Li-Li got married and went to live with her husband and mother-in-law. In a very short time, Li-Li found that she couldn't get along with her mother-in-law at all. Their personalities were very different, and Li-Li was angered by many of her mother-in-law's habits. In addition, she criticised Li-Li constantly.

Days passed days, and weeks passed weeks. Li-Li and her mother-in-law never stopped arguing and fighting. But what made the situation even worse was that, according to ancient Chinese tradition, Li-Li had to bow to her mother-in-law and obey her every wish.

All the anger and unhappiness in the house was causing Li-Li's poor husband great distress. Finally, Li-Li could not stand her mother-in-law's bad temper and dictatorship any longer, and she decided to do something about it.

Li-Li went to see her father's good friend, Mr Huang, who sold herbs. She explained the situation to him and asked if he would give her some poison so that she could solve the problem once and for all. Mr Huang thought for a while, and finally said, 'Li-Li, I will help you solve your problem, but you must listen to me and obey what I tell you.' Li-Li said, 'Yes, Mr Huang, I will do whatever you tell me to do.'

Mr Huang went into the back room, and returned in a few minutes with a package of herbs. He told Li-Li, 'You can't use a quick-acting poison to get rid of your mother-in-law, because that would cause people to become suspicious. Therefore, I have given you a number of herbs that will slowly build up poison in her body. Every other day, prepare some delicious meal and put a little of these herbs in her serving. Now, in order to make sure that nobody suspects you when she dies, you must be very careful to act very friendly towards her. Don't argue with her, obey her every wish and treat her like a queen.'

Li-Li was so happy. She thanked Mr Huang and hurried home to start her plot of murdering her mother-in-law. Weeks went by, months went by, and every other day, Li-Li served the specially treated food to her mother-in-law. She remembered what Mr Huang had said about avoiding suspicion, so she controlled her temper, obeyed her mother-in-law and treated her like her own mother. After six months had passed, the whole household had changed.

Li-Li had practised controlling her temper so much that she found that she almost never got mad or upset. She hadn't had an argument with her mother-in-law in six months, because she now seemed much kinder and easier to get along with. The mother-in-law's attitude towards Li-Li had also changed, and she began to love Li-Li like her own daughter. She kept telling friends and relatives that Li-Li was the best daughter-in-law one could ever find. Li-Li and her mother-in-law were now treating each other like a real mother and daughter. Li-Li's husband was very happy to see what was happening.

One day, Li-Li came to see Mr Huang and asked for his help again. She said, 'Dear Mr Huang, please help me to keep the poison from killing my mother-in-law. She's changed into such a nice woman, and I love her like my own mother. I do not want her to die because of the poison I gave her.'

Mr Huang smiled and nodded his head. 'Li-Li, there's nothing to worry about. I never gave you any poison. The herbs I gave you were vitamins to improve her health. The only poison was in your mind and your attitude towards her, but that has all been washed away by the love that you gave her.'

(Extracted from www.angsuman.taragana.net; the origins of the story are unknown)

Chapter **6**

RUNG 3:
WORK DIVAS WHO STICK TOGETHER?

THE JOY LUCK SISTERHOOD

> 'There is a special place in hell for women who do not help other
> women.'
> — *Madeleine K Albright*
> *(American politician and professor; 1937–?)*

Do the sisters really stick together? What if they are competing for the same man?
Or the same job? Does the sisterhood then fall apart at the seams? Men have a perception of women as a coven of girlfriends, bonding with ease. They also know that
women can be incredibly bitchy towards each other. They don't understand the con-
tradiction. Do we? What about in the workplace? Are things any different there?

Women are generally able to bond more easily than men. Plenty has been written
on the nature of relationships between women, but to summarise much of what has
been said (and to state the obvious), women are more communicative and nurturing
than men. This makes, in my opinion, woman-to-woman interaction twice as effective as woman-to-man communication.

How adept are you at creating bonds? Let's test you in a social setting. Here's the
scenario: You have been invited to a dinner party where there are five couples, all

linked to your man's business. You know only the host couple. The men are happily talking about work, leaving you with the other women. Do you choose any particular person to chat to? If so, on what basis do you choose her? Is it the woman standing closest to you, or the one you know? Maybe it's the woman who looks like you or is nearer your age? Or the one you overhear talking about a subject close to your heart – kids, career, shoes, dogs? Do you just linger around the edges, not involving yourself in the conversation? Do you keep quiet and listen to what everyone has to say but offer little input of your own? Do you take over the conversation? Show them how to drink tequila? Or maybe you muscle in on the men's conversation? (Hint: Your behavioural style will be an influence here.)

Now for the exam: At the end of the evening, with how many of these women have you established a bond? How many will you contact again? How many want to see *you* again? Next time you find yourself in a similar social setting, observe your own behaviour. If you do not bond with at least a couple of the women, sorry, sister, but you need to work on those relationship skills. Good relationships require you to be proactive and reactive for ties to develop.

The way in which you behave in the social environment is a decent predictor of what you are likely to do in the workplace. There is no right or wrong. What you need to be watching is your pattern – and, more interestingly, how you treat the women with whom you do not feel a connection.

A man I had known since junior school, and with whom I was working at the time, had recently divorced and wanted to introduce me to his new girlfriend. Although I was fond of his ex-wife, I had no direct relationship with her. I was introduced to the new lady and my jaw dropped to the floor. She had an incredible body (some of it plastic – not that I have any objection to women making the most of themselves), was dressed to kill (spray-on clothing, glitter make-up) and was able to make intelligent conversation with everyone present.

On the surface, she seemed like a pretty good catch, if flash is your thing. I can't mention her name, as she is quite a high-profile businesswoman and what I am saying is a bit unkind, so let's call her Roxy. I could see Racy Roxy took time and care over her outward appearance, but I wanted to know who she was on the *inside*.

I think I'm pretty reasonable at bonding with other women – I ask them questions, I listen to the answers, I offer personal snippets from my own life – but, try as I might, I could extract no warmth from this woman. I thought that maybe it was just me, so when I next met up with Roxy, I tried to bond again. No luck. I concluded that she was just a bitch. And guess what? Bitch of note.

Why was Racy Roxy reluctant to bond with me? Did she not know how to relate to other women? Was she threatened by me (unlikely – I don't have the million-dollar body and the MBA)? What was it? I think she simply didn't like other women. When I chatted to my mates (not only the girls) about her, they proffered the same conclusion.

Here's a revelation: If you don't like other women, you'll be bad at the sister-hood thing. Sisterhood isn't about being a coven of witches or bitches. It's about being there for each other when we need support, advice, a slap around the head or a shoulder to cry on. Another revelation: Men have a saying: 'What goes on tour stays on tour.' The same needs to apply to the sisters. Keep confidences, relate to other women, and you will be a welcome member of any sisterhood.

In the workplace, diva or not, you will need your work sisters. Times get tough, very tough, and your support group is important in getting you through these moments, hopefully making you stronger along the way. Resist the temptation to form cliques (very bad karma), but be prepared to belong to lots of different sister-hoods. And brotherhoods. Don't identify only with the women – you need to be sure you are included in the mixed groups as well. This brings about balance, or yin and yang, if you prefer. Be equally wary of belonging to only the men's groups, though.

Your groups – your contacts – form the essence of your social network, and as Robert Appelbaum, the most dashing and eligible attorney in South Africa, says, 'Intelligent social networking is the key to success.' You will recognise, from our very posh Diva Investment Needs Hierarchy, that these 'hoods' and groups form an important part of Step C, so pay them the attention they deserve.

THE WICKED WITCH OF WORK

> 'WITCH, n. (1) Any ugly and repulsive old woman, in wicked league with the devil. (2) A beautiful and attractive young woman, in wicked-ness a league beyond the devil.'   — *Ambrose Bierce*
> *(American writer and editor; 1842–1914)*

What happens when the sisters turn against you? When they become the wicked witches of your childhood nightmares?

Firstly, unless you've done something really, really bad, the people who care about you are unlikely to turn against you and become witches. It's the fair-weather friends you need to watch. Secondly, those errant cliques, bitches and witches that emerge along the way will be an unpleasant but temporary terror. Thirdly, if you are one of the witches, beware a central tenet of Wicca, which says that everything you do will come back to you, threefold. Basically, this means that every time you are cruel, selfish, mean, bitchy, deceitful (or, conversely, caring, kind, loving, etc.) to any person, dog, tree, spider or whatever, this act will be returned to you three times.

How do you recognise your true friends and sisters? They're the ones who share your miseries and celebrate your successes: the promotions, pay rises, retrenchments, marriages, divorces, babies, new shoes, bad hats and the like. It is the witches you need to watch out for – especially the ones who present themselves to you as lovely princesses but who are really gnarled and rotten on the inside. They can't hide their inner selves. It will leak out in the form of snide remarks, bitchy comments, gossip...

If you happen along witches in your path, avoid them, ignore them, minimise them. If you are starting to realise that someone you thought was a sister may in fact be a witch, take the pain now and cut the relationship. It will be far less traumatic in the long run. Don't be too unkind (remember the Wiccan curse?), because in many cases the reason for their ugliness is insecurity. Give them a gentle shove in the direction of a psychologist (or exorcist, if they are truly beyond the pale).

With what you now know about behavioural styles, you have probably figured out that insecurity manifests in lots of ways – self-doubt, uncertainty, self-consciousness, jealousy, bitchiness – it's a very long list. Everyone has insecurities of some sort, but it is the degree of severity of that insecurity that helps or hinders a climb up the corporate ladder. Sometimes a little insecurity is just the motivation needed to rise to the top.

If insecurity popped up on *your* list of 'bad', be brave and decide if this is damaging your career or not. If, in your moment of truth, you realise that you are moderately insecure, then chat to a wise friend about it and get some guidance. If it's quite a big issue, maybe a counsellor can help. If it is a demon that is ruining your life, don't be too proud to seek help from a professional (and no, fortune-tellers are not professionals).

A BIT OF A BITCH

> 'When a man gives his opinion, he's a man. When a woman gives her opinion, she's a bitch.'
> — *Bette Davis*
> *(American actress; 1908–1989)*

Bitches are usually fun to be around. They have an endless supply of caustic, catty comments and can keep us amused for hours with the latest 'who's doing what to whom'. And I believe there is a little bit of the bitch in all of us. Some of us control our bitch alter ego better than others, but she's there nonetheless.

Is being a bitch such a bad thing? Well, it depends. We've discussed not being a doormat or a victim, fixing our 'bad' and making difficult life choices, finding mentors to help us learn, controlling our behaviour and overcoming our insecurities – that's a lot of changing for one diva to contemplate. If being a bitch is a bad thing, then surely this, too, must change?

I made the comment 'it depends' if being a bitch is a bad thing or not. Let me explain what I mean. You are who you are and you are fabulous as you are. Sure, there are aspects of your behaviour, including the words you choose, with whom you align yourself, and so on, that may need to be tweaked for you to become a wondrous Work Diva, but you still need to be you. If you have a big bitch inside you that you let out to play often, you will need to make a big change; if you have a big bitch inside you that you don't let out the front door very often, you're likely to have anxiety issues; if you have a little bitch that you let out from time to time, your biggest problem is probably guilt; if you have a little bitch that occasionally sneaks out, you're perfect as you are. And if you have no inner bitch, maybe you are a divine being.

It is important to recognise that while being a bitch can sometimes be fun, this behaviour can really hurt the people around you – which will ultimately hurt you. If, in the work environment, you get a reputation as a bitch, it will not help your climb to the top. If you are a beautiful, desirable bitch who is prepared to manipulate people (for 'people' read men, as other women aren't so easily fooled), you may be able to get to the top, but it's going to take one helluva lot of work for you to stay there. Is it worth it? I certainly don't think so.

So, how do you keep your inner bitch under control? Here are three quick tips:

1. Don't hang around with people who encourage you to be bitchy or who are bitchy themselves (it rubs off!).
2. Think before you speak – if what you want to say will hurt someone, don't say it.
3. Practise being kind. Kindness is the anti-bitch!

Now tuck your inner bitch up in bed, kiss her goodnight and tell her she's going to take a long, long sleep.

WISE WORDS FROM OPRAH WINFREY

'Don't speak evil of someone if you don't know for certain, and if you do know, ask yourself, why am I telling it?'
– Johann Kaspar Lavater (Swiss theologian, poet and physiognomist; 1741–1801)

Talking about sisters, witches and bitches, here is a fabulous article written by Oprah Winfrey on the subject of gossip.

What I Know For Sure by Oprah Winfrey, taken from *O Magazine*, July 2006

I've always been a homebody. I know that might be hard to believe, given my full schedule, but I usually head home right after work, finish dinner before 7, and climb into bed by 9:30 P.M. Even on weekends, home is my all-time favourite hangout. Since I've spent most of my adult life in the public eye, it's important for me to carve out a private space. A refuge. A safe house.

I know first-hand just how hurtful negative words can be. Early in my career, when the tabloids began printing so many untruthful things about me, I was devastated ... And I wasted a lot of energy worrying about whether people would believe the falsehoods. How could they get away with printing outright slander? I had to fight the urge to call up anyone who'd maligned me and defend myself.

That was before I understood what I now know for sure: When someone spreads lies about you, you're not in it. Never. Gossip – be it in the form of a rumour that's sweeping the nation or a gripe session between friends – reflects the insecurity of those who initiate it ...

In short, gossip is an assassination attempt by a coward ...

What would happen if we declared our homes, our relationships, our lives a gossip-free zone? We'd probably be surprised at how much time we'd free up to do the work that's most significant – building our dreams rather than tearing down others'. We'd fill our homes with a spirit of truth that makes visitors want to kick off their shoes and stay awhile. And we'd remember that while words have the power to destroy, they also have the power to heal.

Oprah Winfrey has also spoken about the 'Three Filter Test' (origin unknown; sometimes credited to Socrates), which suggests you ask three questions of any information you are about to 'pass on':
– Are you certain the information is true?
– Is it something *good* about someone?
– Is it useful?

If you answer 'no' to even one of these questions, then you should not pass on the information, because it is probably nothing more than gossip. Think before you speak, before you gossip, dear Work Diva.

Chapter 7

RUNG 4:
A WORK DIVA OF ART AND SUBSTANCE

THE ART OF IMPRESSIONS

'You cannot climb the ladder of success dressed in the costume of
failure.'   *– Hilary Hinton, aka Zig Ziglar*
(American author and motivator; 1926–?)

Your climb up the ladder can be hampered, even damaged, by the company you keep.
People notice with whom you choose to align yourself – it affects their impressions
of you and the decisions the big bosses make about your career. So, steer clear of
the coven of witches, watch out for the litters of bitches and focus on your sisters,
your mentor and your fabulous self.

This takes us right back to Step A of our Diva Investment Needs Hierarchy –
physical appearance and impressions. How important are they? Do first impressions really count? There is an old adage that says one should not judge a book by
its cover, but the message behind this saying is to discourage people from forming
quick opinions, because that is exactly what we are inclined to do – which means,
basically, first impressions are very important.

Want to be the Work Diva? Well, then, you need to look and act the part! The
clothes you choose, your grooming in general, the words you use, the books you
read, the company you keep – all these, and more, contribute to creating impressions

63

that influence the way in which other people perceive you. If you pitch up at work looking like you've been out on the town all night, what does that say about you? Will it help get you promoted? Even if you *have* been out razzling all night, you need to do the best you can with the damaged goods.

If you're serious about your career, send out this message via your appearance as much as in your behaviour and hard work. You are what you wear. Your clothes do a lot of gossiping about you behind your back. I'm not, for one moment, suggesting that you need to rush off and buy designer labels – they count for nothing if your shoes aren't polished or there's a stain on your shirt. The books and articles available on 'dressing for success' are usually very good, so start reading. Alternatively, you could hire an image consultant or personal dresser, but that costs money, honey.

Here are ten tips (I discovered the dos and don'ts the hard way) for dressing like a Work Diva in the business context:

1. You need a few good-quality items in your wardrobe. One great skirt and jacket and a few fab shirts can go a very long way.
2. If you have a limited wardrobe or budget, go for colours that you can easily mix and match. A lot of big stores have a 'work-wear' section that makes this easier.
3. If you are addicted to bright colours, wear only one item of clothing (preferably a less obtrusive item) and one accessory that is a loud colour.
4. On the subject of accessories, too many is simply too many. Choose fewer, better quality, more tasteful items.
5. Avoid the latest fad fashions – you want to be taken seriously, not seen as a clothes horse.
6. I'm not a fan of masculine 'power' suits. When a woman walks into my office dressed in a smart yet feminine suit or a stylish, more formal outfit, I think, 'Here's a confident woman,' rather than 'Here's a ball-busting *über*-bitch.'
7. Dress like a tart and you are the tart. Don't be surprised when you get a pinched bum rather than a promotion.
8. Treat yourself to a fabulous classic handbag. It goes wherever you go, so make it one with which you are proud to be seen.

9. If you are going to waste your money, waste it on shoes. Don't you just love shoes? Don't they always make you feel better? And no matter how much weight you gain, your shoes always fit!

10. Take pride in your appearance. Always wear clean clothes. It's fine to be dressed in the same dress or skirt or whatever twice in a week, if it's still clean, but be sure not to wear it on consecutive days!

Don't forget to pay due attention to your hair, your make-up and the rest of you. Even if you don't care about clothes or make-up, it's no excuse for not presenting the best possible you. Make those first impressions count, because your appearance and the impressions you create, like it or not, influence many facets of your career. Here's an example: Did you know that even your weight impacts your professional prospects?

The Obesity Society recently published research on their website (www.obesity. org) that says:

> *Experimental studies have found that when a resume is accompanied by a picture or video of an overweight person (compared to an 'average' weight person), the overweight applicant is rated more negatively and is less likely to be hired. Other research shows that overweight employees are ascribed multiple negative stereotypes including being lazy, sloppy, less competent, lacking in self-discipline, disagreeable, less conscientious, and poor role models. In addition, overweight employees may suffer wage penalties, as they tend to be paid less for the same jobs, are more likely to have lower paying jobs, and are less likely to get promoted than thin people with the same qualifications.*

No, it's not fair, but we've already spoken about life and unfairness. Take control of what you can control, and your appearance *is* a controllable factor.

If we are indeed the impressions we create, we need to maximise what we present. Coco Chanel, the French fashion designer, said, 'A girl should be two things: classy and fabulous.'

FROM IMPRESSIONS TO SUBSTANCE

'Fashion can be bought. Style one must possess.'
– Edna Woolman Chase
(American editor in chief of Vogue *from 1914 to 1952)*

We've established that people judge others based on their appearance. It is only after the initial impression has been created that we find out what the person is *really* like. But what if you are never given the opportunity to present the real you? Back to reality – you need to take time and care with your appearance. It's important, whether you like it or not.

If you feel all this appearance stuff is a bit too shallow for your liking, this is where Step B of our Diva Investment Needs Hierarchy kicks in – attitude. The good news is that impressions are driven by appearance *and* your general air or attitude. Mostly appearance, but attitude does count too. If you think you are Ugly Betty, then you *are* Ugly Betty. If you feel more Kate Moss, then that is who you become. How you feel on the inside is projected, mostly unwittingly, on the outside. Others pick up the signals that you, often unconsciously, send.

My husband Simon and I were in Paris recently, celebrating our first anniversary (after four years of marriage – but that's a story for later). We treated ourselves to a stay at Hotel de Sers and, as we were checking out of the hotel, a glamorous young woman swept past us. She was attractive, well (not exceptionally) dressed, with a bounce in her step and a smile on her face. What caught my attention, though, wasn't her prettiness or her clothing – it was her general air of confidence. As she stepped out of the hotel, flashbulbs started popping and I realised she must be a celebrity of some sort. The hotel discreetly confirmed that she was 'famous', but wouldn't tell me who she was. My fifteen-year-old nephew Daniel Meredith says it might have been one of the members of Destiny's Child, maybe Michelle Williams. I bumped into the actor David Morse in London recently. Same story.

What 'air' do you present? Diva or doormat? Do you skulk, shuffle or scowl, or do you hold your head high and smile at the world? What is your posture like? Pull back your shoulders, suck in your tummy and stick out your breasts (this also helps you to immediately 'lose' two kilograms!). Taking pride in yourself and your appearance impacts the way others see you, but, more importantly, how you see yourself. Project fabulous you in your posture, grooming, self-possession and confidence, and the world sees a diva. Helena Rubenstein, the Polish-born American cosmetics tycoon, said, 'There are no ugly women – only lazy ones.'

In understanding, and accepting, the role that appearance and attitude play in telling tales about you, it's time now to look at what happens next – that which lies beyond the superficial. How do you become a Work Diva of substance?

THE SCIENCE OF SUBSTANCE

> 'If you want to be respected by others, the great thing is to respect yourself. Only by that, only by self-respect will you compel others to respect you.'
> — *Fyodor Dostoevsky*
> *(Russian novelist and writer; 1821–1881)*

Creating a positive impression is an important first step, but this impression needs to be supported with substance – Step D of our Diva Investment Needs Hierarchy. Credibility, delivery, consistency, industry, honesty, reliability, responsibility and respect – these are a few of the elements that constitute the depth of substance the Work Diva needs to exhibit in her climb to the top of the ladder.

Which of the 'substance' roll-call items above do you think is the most important factor from a Work Diva's point of view? If you said 'respect', you guessed right (or you looked at the Diva Investment Needs Hierarchy again). Either way, well done! Respect is defined as being worthy of esteem, or being regarded with honour. This basically means that your credibility, delivery, consistency and the other traits mentioned become meaningful only if they are reinforced by respect.

That's all well and good, but what actually needs to be *done* to earn respect? Is there anything the Work Diva can do that will guarantee her the respect of those around her, without selling her soul? Here is a list of ten really important attributes that are sure to secure you respect and boost your climb up the corporate ladder. And the great thing about them is that you can practise them at home, with your friends, on your man, family, pets, bosses, enemies – you name it!

Ten sure-fire ways to establish credibility and earn respect:

1. Under-promise and over-deliver

Don't disappoint others by saying you will get something to them on a certain date or to a certain quality and then deliver less than they were expecting. Even if you do the very best you can, delivering less always puts you in a bad light. Rather set the right expectation of what you can deliver, and by when, at the beginning of any assignment, and then pleasantly surprise those around you by exceeding this expectation whenever possible.

2. Get things finished

One of the women with whom my organisation works is Patricia Martins, an executive with the local operation of a global information technology (IT) company. I call Patricia 'The Girl Who Gets Things Done'. If Patricia says she will do something, she does it. She sees assignments through to completion, regardless of the challenges and obstacles she encounters. Too many people simply give up when the going gets tough and justify their failure to finish the job with a myriad excuses and justifications. There is a difference between knowing when to throw in the towel vs throwing it in because the going got too tough. Patricia understands the difference and consistently delivers results. I would hire Patricia in a heartbeat.

3. Be consistent

People want predictability – not someone who charms one minute and then flies into a rage or a sulk the next. Your big bosses, certainly, will promote the divas on whom they can depend, not those who are up one minute and down the next. We all have our moods and moments, our PMS and other catastrophes, but the more you can regulate these in the work environment, the bigger the favour you'll be doing yourself. Remember, it is possible to control *your* behaviour, even if you can't control the behaviour of others.

4. Work hard *and* work smart

Working hard is not enough. Sure, you will have to work very hard indeed in your climb to the top (and even more so when you get to the top), but it is never enough. A secretary who works hard will gain a reputation for being a great secretary, but is it enough to get her a director's job? Unfortunately, no. You need to be working hard and smart *at the same time*. But what does 'working smart' mean? It's knowing how to prioritise, where best to invest your energy and limited resources, understanding the difference between what's urgent and what's important, being able to delegate appropriately and the like. If you're not sure how to work smarter, ask your mentor – that's what he or she is there for, after all.

5. Say what you mean and mean what you say

Get to the point. In business, nothing is more irritating than someone who dithers or uses fifty words when fifteen would suffice (I'm inclined to go the other way and use too few words – I guess it's because I'm a Driver). This does not mean that you shouldn't explain things properly; it just means thinking about what you want to say, how to say it and then saying it. Keep your communication – whether oral or written – clear, concise and honest. And say what you mean – don't be duplicitous or deceitful or a clever Dick. People need to be able to rely on what you say, so don't say things you don't mean. Think before you speak. The powers that be will be far more impressed with someone who is open, articulate and to the point than some dithering, vague punster.

6. Keep your word

As part of building respect, people need to be able to take you at your word. If you make a promise to do something or be somewhere, make sure that that is what you do, even if it means you are inconvenienced. People set huge store by the promises of others, so doing everything in your power to be known as someone upon whom others can depend – someone who keeps their promises – will serve you very well in your climb up the ladder.

7. Tell the truth, despite the consequences

Where do you draw the line? Do you convince yourself that it's okay to tell a little white lie if it spares someone's feelings? What if it's a big lie to protect someone you love? I always try to tell the truth (partly because I can't remember the lies and get easily caught out), but when telling the truth will hurt someone, I choose my words very carefully. Nobody respects a liar, whether you are lying to someone else – regardless of the motive – or to yourself. Lying to yourself very quickly translates into a victim mentality. Be honest and be open – it makes for a much simpler life!

8. Take responsibility

This operates on two levels – accepting responsibility in the form of the duties or roles expected of you, and then taking responsibility for your actions. In accepting responsibility, you will be getting the credit if the project is a success, but also carrying the blame if it all goes horribly wrong. You can have both, or none. Your choice. Only a victim tries to take one (you know which one) without the other. In building respect, you need to be seen as willing to take on responsibility – especially responsibility that stretches you – and the incumbent knocks or kudos that go with an assignment. Can you do it?

9. Don't be afraid to make the difficult decisions

Many people battle with making decisions, never mind taking the unpopular ones. Decision-making, like most other business skills and talents, can be learnt. Attend a course, read books, discuss the decisions with your mentor. 'But *how* does one make a difficult or unpopular decision?,' I hear you ask. Well, it comes back to the truth. Be true to yourself. You owe it to yourself – and to the people who will be impacted by your decision – to think through all the options, consequences and outcomes. If you then make a decision you believe in your heart to be the right one, you will be okay. Even if it all goes pop, you'll be able to justify (even if only to your-self) the basis of the decision and so protect your standing. Any difficult decision can be accompanied by fallout we would prefer to avoid. Just be brave. Making the hard decisions is incredibly empowering.

10. Treat others with respect

Do you show respect to other people? Think about how you treat the waiters in a restaurant or the cleaners in a public loo. Many people try to elevate themselves by treating the 'little people' badly, but all they're really showing is that they lack manners and grace. The most impressive business people and leaders I have met all have this one thing in common – graciousness. Grace is the ability to show someone respect without being servile or obsequious. Grace comes across as good manners. Being on time illustrates not only professionalism, but respect for the other person's time. If it is good enough for Nelson Mandela, it's good enough for me. If you treat others with disrespect, don't be surprised when you are treated in the same contemptuous manner.

While the suggestions above may seem like well-worn platitudes, it's because they are common truths that you have heard plenty of times before. Did you pick up the common thread between the points? If so, you will have noticed that consistency, reliability and trustworthiness cropped up time and again. These are the respect-based qualities a Work Diva needs to climb the ladder all the way to the top, without selling her soul along the way.

WORDS OF WISDOM

'I would be most content if my children grew up to be the kind of people who think decorating consists mostly of building enough bookshelves.'
— *Anna Quindlen*
(American author and journalist; 1952–?)

You may well, by now, be asking lots of 'how' questions – how do I fix this or change that or do the substance thing? The answers lie, dear diva, in books.

During a high-end deal-making course my company conducted recently, the executive who had booked the programme for his team asked me to compile a reading list for his group. I was flattered to be asked to do this by a man I consider to be extremely well read, but it put me in a difficult position – which books should I recommend? As I have pushed the issue of reading and learning quite hard, I thought it would be useful if I included a list of recommended reading in *Work Diva*.

A few points about the list. Firstly, my list of business books would be a bit short, given my low boredom threshold with these, so I coerced my wonderfully erudite husband Simon to help me compile the list (his input also brings balance to the list). Secondly, the list below is *recommended* reading, which means you need to use your judgement as to whether these books would make suitable reading for you or not. Thirdly, one needs to read widely to have a decent grounding, so the list below extends beyond merely business books. The books are listed in no particular order.

The business books I recommend:
1. *Blue Ocean Strategy* by W Chan Kim and Renée Mauborgne
2. *The Trusted Advisor* by David H Maister, Robert Galford and Charles Green
3. *Competitive Advantage* by Michael E Porter
4. *Competitive Strategy* by Michael E Porter
5. *Freakonomics* by Steven D Levitt and Stephen J Dubner
6. *Strategic Selling* by Robert Miller and Stephen Heiman
7. *The Art of Woo* by G Richard Shell and Mario Moussa
8. *Trump-Style Negotiation* by George H Ross
9. *Kiss, Bow or Shake Hands* by Terri Morrison and Wayne A Conway
10. *When Cultures Collide* by Richard D Lewis

The business books Simon recommends:
1. *Good to Great* by Jim Collins
2. *Socrates and the Fox* by Clem Sunter and Chantell Ilbury
3. *The Art of War* by Thomas Cleary
4. *The Tipping Point* by Malcolm Gladwell
5. *The Fifth Discipline* by Peter M Senge
6. *The Dip* by Seth Godin

Non-fiction reading that has had an impact on my personal and business life includes:

1. *Quirkology* by Richard Wiseman
2. *Personality Plus* by Florence Littauer
3. *The Wheel of Life* by Elisabeth Kübler-Ross
4. *Journey of Souls* by Michael Newton
5. *The Five Love Languages* by Gary Chapman
6. *The Architecture of All Abundance* by Lenedra Jewel Carroll

Simon's favourite non-fiction and biographical history books:

1. *The Monk Who Sold His Ferrari* by Robin S Sharma
2. *Living the 80/20 Way* by Richard Koch
3. *The Crucible* by Dr Don Beck and Graham Linscott
4. *Man's Search for Meaning* by Viktor E Frankl
5. *Country of My Skull* by Antjie Krog
6. *Dispatches* by Michael Herr
7. *Blood, Toil, Tears and Sweat: The Great Speeches of Winston Churchill*, edited by David Cannadine

Happy reading!

Chapter 8

RUNG 5:
THE WORK DIVA'S WICKED WAY WITH WORDS

COMMUNICATION IS A DIVA'S BEST FRIEND

> 'We women talk too much; nevertheless we only say half of what
> we know.'   *— Viscountess Nancy Witcher Astor*
> *(British politician; 1879–1964)*

On the subject of words, we've spent a lot of time, so far, taking long, hard looks at our behaviour. It's time now for a close-up with another element of conduct that is well within our control: Communication. Women are supposed to be the stronger of the sexes when it comes to communication, right? Well, then, why does so much go so wrong? The way in which we communicate, the things we say, the things we *don't* say, the words we use – these all have an impact on the people around us.

A bit of context before we continue. Communication, simply put, is the imparting or exchanging of information. Communication is essentially divided into verbal and non-verbal. According to www.wikipedia.com, verbal communication is concerned with words and includes speech, sign language and writing, whereas non-verbal communication is understood to be communication through wordless messages such as gestures, body language, posture, facial expressions, eye contact, and even your choice of clothes, shoes, accessories and so on.

Much as you can control your behaviour, you can also control your communication – right down to the very words you use and the methods you choose. Words are the symbols of language, and language is the essence of verbal communication. To be able to control your messages effectively, you need to slow down your speech, rather than speed it up, so that you can choose the right words to present the most effective message. The written word draws its power from the fact that the writer has had time to think about what she wants to say. When a person is a powerful oral communicator, it is because she is able to choose her words much more quickly in the moment – not because she has 'the gift of the gab'. I believe it was former President George W Bush's inability to express himself spontaneously and off the cuff that revealed his real level of intelligence.

My husband Simon is reading *Blood, Toil, Tears and Sweat: The Great Speeches of Winston Churchill* edited by David Cannadine. Sir Winston Churchill *(British prime minister; 1874–1965)* was, in my opinion, one of the best orators of the last century. Churchill believed that a single hour of speech took him *weeks* to prepare and write. It was Churchill who said, 'I'm just preparing my impromptu remarks.'

How much time do you spend planning what you are going to say to someone and how you are going to say it? Or do you rush in like the proverbial fool? In telling you the following little secret, I am probably opening myself up to be committed to an asylum, but here goes anyway.

I have conversations in my head, all the time. Every day, much of the day. Conversations with people I know, as well as with people I have never met. Conversations with loved ones, acquaintances, people who are dead or far away, those I want to compliment or criticise. I have the meetings that I am scheduled to have in my head for days before they happen. I talk to my dogs, the trees, flowers. No, smart-ass, they don't answer me back (except for the dogs, of course) – I present both sides of the discussion. I put forward my best arguments or retorts, their likely responses, what I'll say back, and on it goes.

The conversations are about philosophy, values, current affairs, opinions. Sometimes important, and often banal, subjects. I have been having these conversations since I was a kid. I think they started when I realised that I needed to prepare for arguments or discussions with my father. They just never stopped. I hope I don't get to the point where I start having them aloud!

We'll spend a lot of time talking about the words you choose in a moment, but in whatever you say, be sincere. Because communication operates on two levels – the verbal and the non-verbal – people can pick up when you are being insincere. The last thing you need as you climb the ladder of success is to develop a reputation for being disingenuous. Build trust through your communication, which means: Say what you mean and mean what you say. The more eloquently you can do this, the more favourably you'll be considered when it comes to promotion time.

Your written language, however, is just as critical as your oral language. The good thing about writing is that you get to think about what you want to say before you say it. Take care with what you put in writing, though – it sticks around a lot longer than your spoken words. So, if you embarrass yourself, it's there for the whole world to see for a very long time.

Written communication is becoming increasingly important. We're communicating in writing more now than at any other point in history – think the internet, e-mail, text messages, etc. In years gone by, you may have been able to get away with poor writing skills, but now every wannabe Work Diva will be measured by them. If you want to climb to the top, your pen is (not penis) going to help get you there.

Here are five common-sense guidelines for written communication:

1. Write like an adult. Smiley faces and chatspeak (used for text messages) are fine for your mates, but do they belong in business?

2. The written vs the oral forms of communication each have a different impact on the recipient. What may *sound* okay does not always *look* okay. 'I'm cool with it' may sound acceptable, but put this in writing and you come across as the village idiot.

3. If you are responding to someone in anger, write what you want to say, sleep on it – a day, maybe two – then reread and edit your letter or e-mail, and only then send it off. I generally regret e-mails I send in anger – and they are there forever to remind me of my knee-jerk reactions.

4. Be wary of familiarity. E-mails that start with 'Hi girls' or 'Hi all' or something similar, and end with 'Love, Soozee' or the like, are okay in peer-to-peer communication, but are not suitable for your superiors. One of the biggest mistakes people make in business is assuming the familiarity and power of their bosses. I know of a woman who lost her job as an executive assistant because of an e-mail to the executives that began, 'Hello, boys.'

5. Watch out for Facebook. Did you know that there are an increasing number of executives who do research on Facebook before they make someone a job offer? Do you really want your prospective (or, heaven forbid, current) boss seeing you doing a Britney on the internet? No, I didn't think so.

Whereas words are the symbols of verbal communication, body language is the core of non-verbal communication. I'm no body language specialist (there are plenty of experts and good books available on the subject), but what concerns me about body language is that it is very strongly tied to culture. One perfectly acceptable gesture in one country may be a huge insult in another – as I found to my horror when I was working in Egypt. For me, words are a more reliable communication mechanism than body language. Non-verbal communication is transmitted and received, in the main, unconsciously, so you have little or no control over it. Language and words, on the other hand, can be far more easily controlled.

Most of us have had to learn another language at some point. When we speak, albeit badly, in that other language, we choose our words carefully. We may choose the wrong words, but we choose them nonetheless. This makes us think more about what we want to say, so, even when speaking in a foreign tongue, we find power in our oral communication. We need to apply the same forethought to our mother tongue.

Is communication one of a woman's greatest strengths? It can be, but we need to be careful not to multitask while we communicate. If we focus on the discussions in which we're involved, rather than thinking about a million other things at the same time, communication can be our greatest advantage. Think before you speak, listen actively to what is being said, watch for the non-verbal clues and trust your instincts.

WORDS LOST IN TRANSLATION

'In Taiwan, the translation of the Pepsi slogan "Come alive with the Pepsi Generation" came out as "Pepsi will bring your ancestors back from the dead."'   – *Extracted from www.goodquotes.info*

It's time to have a closer look at choosing your words. This is just as important as choosing your Choos. When I talk about 'words', I mean both the oral and written variety and your ability to communicate using these forms of language. I'm also assuming you have a reasonable grasp of language – if you're reading this book, you are just fine.

In presenting The Dealdiva™ programme for women, my organisation spends a disproportionate amount of time focusing on which words to use when doing business deals. Carefully chosen words enable timid women to be more assertive, antagonistic women to tone down their aggression, and everyone to have more control over the selling and negotiating processes that profoundly affect their lives. We show how the correct use of words will help you to get what you want. Guess which word, we believe, holds more power than any other word? Guess which is the most overused word? The answers are at the end of this section.

There is enormous power in words – they can harm and they can heal, they can redeem and condemn, they can get you what you want or stop you in your tracks. They are said but not always heard, listened to but often misinterpreted. They make bad situations bearable and unbearable situations either better, or even worse. I'm sure you get the picture. Do you have a way with words?

My husband Simon is a linguistic genius. In Grade 7 he corrected his English teacher when she said that the word 'susurration', which he'd used in an essay, did not exist. When he brought in his father's giant dictionary to prove her wrong, he had the living daylights beaten out of him for his trouble. He sees a dictionary as 'a bit of light reading, a useful book'. If you're in Simon's league, you no doubt already understand the power words can hold. We lesser mortals desperately need to think before we speak.

Robin Allott, an author and expert on the subject of language and words, wrote a paper ('papers' are how academics and intellectuals measure their worth) titled 'The Power of Words' for the Language Origins Society, Amsterdam, in 1990. In this fascinating paper (you can read the full paper on www.percepp.demon.co. uk), Robin Allott has the following to say (edited):

What I want to emphasise is the unrecognised power of words. The value of the individual word. We take words – language – very much for granted, just as we take our eyes, our power of vision for granted. But both are tremendously flexible with wide-ranging powers – which have hardly been described in any complete way, never mind explained. Language is a powerful instrument. It is used in many different ways and constitutes one of the principal forces controlling and forming human behaviour. Besides its most familiar and normally most discussed use, communication, language is important through its use in one's private thought, in science and in oratory, in poetry, in philosophy – and perhaps most remarkably in techniques of hypnosis.

Do you remember the movie *Taking Care of Business* (it was titled *Filofax* in South Africa) with James Belushi? James Belushi's character, a loveable thief called Jimmy, finds a Filofax in which there is a list of 'power' words – 'first-rate, phenomenal, superlative, benevolent'. After reading the list, Jimmy goes on to tell someone that he looks 'very benevolent today'. You can create a list of 'power' words if you like, but if you use them incorrectly, you, too, can look like a right nana.

Rather than making lists of wondrous words, make a promise to yourself to think before you speak. Yes, it means that you need to plan what you're going to say, right down to the very words you'll use. Practise saying what you need or want to say but please, whatever you do, don't learn the script off by heart. Why not? Because the person with whom you'll be having the conversation doesn't have their side of the script, so when the discussion veers away from yours – as it is guaranteed to do – you'll be lost. Think, plan, practise, and then engage. That's all you need to do.

By now you're probably muttering, 'Sure, that's easy for you to say.' Let's talk about what *you* need to do to improve the manner in which you use words.

First, take a look at your behavioural style. As a Driver, when someone I know walks into my office for the first time in a day, I find myself saying, 'Have you done …?' Not: 'Hello and how are you?' Other expressions I tend to use are, 'You must do this' or 'You need to …' rather than phrases such as, 'It could be to your benefit if you …' or 'Have you considered …?' One of my friends, George Oertel (you may know his name if you're into cycling – he was the 2008 South African Vet B Cross Country Champion), is forever correcting my phraseology. It drives him nuts when I make statements such as 'The Dealmaker™ course is fantastic.' He thinks I should be saying 'In my opinion, The Dealmaker™ course is fantastic.' I get far too much of a kick out of driving him mental to change this, even though I know he is right.

Just a quick look at your own behavioural style will give you clues as to what adjustments you may need to make to the way in which you use words. If you are constantly being misinterpreted or misunderstood, the problem lies squarely in your corner. But, luckily, it's something you can fix.

Next, remember we made a list of our 'good' and 'bad' attributes? You need to … (there I go again!). Correction. It would be of real benefit to you if you did the same exercise with your 'good' and 'bad' words. Decide which words you want to keep and which you want to let go; start practising and correcting yourself. Ask someone – anyone who won't tease you – to help you reprogramme the part of your brain ('Simon says' it's the prefrontal lobes of the neocortex) that controls your words and language formation. Get them ('ask' them, Kim) please to point out to you when you are using words you want to eradicate from your vocabulary.

Lastly, research, read, read some more, and more again, on the role and impact of words, language and communication on your life and your career. For a list of great books on these subjects, see www.amazon.com/Books-for-Communication-Self-Growth-Happiness/lm/4DPOLHOCE5VN. There are also fun books like *Eats, Shoots & Leaves* by Lynne Truss. Words can be enormously entertaining!

Here are the answers to the questions I posed earlier:
- The most powerful word in the world? 'If'
- The most overused word? 'I'

I SWEAR IT'S NOT ME

''Twas but my tongue, 'twas not my soul that swore.'
– Euripides (Greek writer of tragedy; 480–406 BC)

As much as I love words, I love swearing. It's kind of emancipating, don't you think? I do most of it under my breath, but from time to time the bad words slip out. The hypocrisy is that I am often uncomfortable when people I don't know, particularly women, swear in front of me. Social norms dictate that men shouldn't swear in mixed company and that ladies should not swear at all – but we do! My friends and I take great delight in the liberation swearing brings. The truth is that most people see swearing as crass – not a desirable label for an aspiring Work Diva.

'Words are, of course, the most powerful drug used by mankind,' said Rudyard Kipling, the English author, but where and when is swearing acceptable in business? The Irish swear with impunity. I was coaching a group of course delegates in London a few years ago and pulled up an Irishman named Fergal for swearing in a business session. He was bemused. 'Feck is not a swearword,' he chirped. 'My mother uses it all the time, and she is so straight she thinks I was born by immaculate conception.' How could I argue with that?

I was at a train station in Chester in England recently when a few young thugs, of both sexes, got off the train and started pushing people around, generally making a nuisance of themselves. It was their foul mouths that struck me most. I vowed never to swear again. It lasted a couple of months, but it made me think. If I swear in the business environment, do those present perceive me in the same light as I did the yobs at the train station?

I did a little research and found an interesting article titled 'To Swear Is Human, and At Least for Some, to Curse Is Divine' by Natalie Angier, published in the *International Herald Tribune*, September 2005. Here is an extract from the article (edited):

Researchers who study the evolution of language and the psychology of swearing say that cursing is a human universal. Every language, dialect or patois ever studied, whether living or dead, spoken by millions or by a single small tribe, turns out to have its share of forbidden speech.

Men's Health magazine recently included an article on swearing written by Dr Cliff Arnell, a psychologist specialising in communication and stress (and about whom I could find nothing on the internet):

I've seen the mood drop in many meetings when, after the usual pleasantries, someone drops an F-word into the conversation. Be it unconsciously or to show off, people will see it as unattractive and as a sign of low intelligence. We usually know when it's not okay to swear, but sometimes we can get into bad habits. The key to avoiding problems is to reset your programming. You need to unlearn inappropriate lessons.

Although interesting, the article makes the assumption that we know when swearing is and is not appropriate. I, for one, am not sure I can differentiate, so I decided to write a list of three rules for those of us who get a fix from swearing *à la* Rudyard Kipling:

1. Don't swear in the business environment; that way you can't get yourself into trouble.
2. See Rule 1.
3. See Rule 1.

The research I have conducted into the power of words is, for me, the determinant on whether we should swear or not. And I think not. I will continue to swear in the company of my close friends who, hopefully, don't judge me, but I will no longer swear in the business environment. Then again, is 'shit' a swearword, or has it fallen into common, everyday usage? I don't know – use your judgement – but 'when in doubt, don't' is probably the sensible advice.

FROM LISTENING TO QUESTIONING

'Listening well and answering well is one of the greatest perfections that can be obtained in conversation.'

– François de La Rochefoucauld
(French classical writer; 1613–1680)

Effective communication is essentially a balance – a balance between talking and listening and watching. Watching relates to body language, to the subtle interplays between the people in a room and to observing reactions during conversations. It was Epictetus (ca. AD 55–135), the ancient Greek Stoic philosopher, who said, 'We have two ears and one mouth so that we can listen twice as much as we speak.' How much time do you spend listening? Is it two thirds of the interaction, or are you so busy waiting to get your words into the conversations that you don't actually hear what's being said?

Try to 'be in the moment', as the New Age philosophers like to say. Be fully present – listen to the words being used and to their context. Don't start thinking about what to cook for dinner, or how to rebut the argument being presented, or that you should have bought the red pair too. Listen. Pause. Think. Speak.

Information is power. What is the best and most reliable way of getting information? Asking questions! If two thirds of our time is meant to be spent listening, half of the time left should be spent asking questions. Believe it or not, people like to be asked questions – especially about themselves. There are plenty of clichés associated with questions. Ask and ye shall receive. If you don't ask, you don't get. And so on and on. Here's a new one for you: Never be afraid to ask for information, no matter how sensitive the subject matter.

The coaches who work with me in delivering The Dealmaker™ programmes have great fun thinking up the most outrageous questions they can ask the delegates on the courses. A favourite is to ask someone – bearing in mind that this person will be answering in front of a whole bunch of strangers – how many different sexual partners they have had. Do you know that most people are willing to disclose this?

The coach will stop the delegate before she can open her closet (well, usually), but it certainly drives home the point. People will answer almost any question you ask them if you ask it directly, unexpectedly and without bad intentions.

In the business context, we are afraid to ask customers to whom we are selling for their budget; they, in turn, don't ask us for our profit margins. When it comes to questions about money, people get very coy. You owe it to yourself to ask the questions: Let the person you are asking decide whether she wants to answer or not.

Do you know how to block a question that you don't want to answer? Saying, 'I am not prepared to answer that' gives far too many clues to the asker about the possible answer. (If you ask someone for their profit margin on an item and they say, 'I am not prepared to disclose that,' you can be sure that the profit is high. If it was low, they'd probably be inclined to share the information.) So, how do you block a question you don't want to answer? If you are thinking 'with another question', you'd be absolutely correct! Just say, 'Why do you want to know that?' or 'Why is that information important to you?' and the question will usually go away. The easiest way to distract someone is to ask them about themselves. And, here's the crazy part – they will love you for it!

If you don't know what is going on or what someone means, remember the story of Fritz. Best you find out what's up as quickly as you can by asking, listening, pausing, and only then speaking. Anthony Robbins, the American author and speaker, said, 'The way we communicate with others and with ourselves ultimately determines the quality of our lives.' Nothing could be more appropriate for the Work Diva – or is that 'word' diva?

LISTENING TO INTUITION

'A woman uses her intelligence to find reasons to support her intuition.'
– *GK Chesterton (British author; 1874–1936)*

We've looked at verbal language and body language, but what role does intuition or 'sixth sense' play in communication? Very simple: Trust your gut. We tend to ignore our gut instincts because we aren't able to explain or measure them. Just because you can't put into words what you are sensing does not mean that your intuition is wrong.

I'm a bit nervous of making far-reaching or life-changing decisions based solely on gut feelings, but that doesn't mean I ignore them. I do factor these instincts into my decisions. If I get a 'feeling' that I need to change roads while I'm driving, I change roads. Too many times I've ignored my intuition and too many times have I said, 'I should have listened.' The same applies to communication. If you get a feeling that what is being said is different from what you *sense* is being said, you are probably right. Listen more carefully. Watch for the non-verbal clues to help you figure out what is really going on. This leaves less and less time for talking. Good thing.

Kim Winser, OBE and businesswoman extraordinaire, made the following comment at an international conference recently: 'My gut is one of my best friends. Sometimes you just "know" your brand, and your instinct guides you to make a common-sense decision. The worst thing to do is to make no decision at all.'

An article titled 'Much More than Just a Pretty Face' by Anton Ferreira in the *Business Times Careers* section of the *Sunday Times* in July 2008 endorsed the instinct to trust our instincts. The article had the following to say on the subject: '[Lindie Engelbrecht, chief executive of the Institute of Directors]: "Women read people a lot better, women have the ability to equal out the aggression in a board situation, they understand marketing products."'

If intuition is good enough for an OBE-winning business maestro and the chief executive of the Institute of Directors, then it has to be good enough for us Work Divas.

Chapter 9

RUNG 6:
BEING WITH THE POWERS THAT BE

BLOCKERS, MR BIG AND YOU

> 'You can't push anyone up the ladder unless he is ready to climb himself.' *– Andrew Carnegie (American industrialist and philanthropist; 1835–1919)*

This is one of the most important rungs of your ladder as you climb towards the top – how to present yourself to, and impress, the executives in whose hands (so to speak) your diva fate rests. I'm talking about the people who decide on whether you are promoted, praised, raised, fired or – even worse – ignored.

As you climb, it will be necessary to set yourself in front of some pretty high-ranking people in your organisation. The first senior person with whom you will interface regularly will be your boss. If you are planning to rise to the very top of your company, the sooner those who will determine or influence your career path know your name, the better. If this is your boss, great; but if your boss is not at the top of the pile, you are going to have to make sure that you start developing relationships with people who are more senior than your boss. This can be tricky.

Why is it so important to access the most senior people in your organisation?

Let me explain with an example. Let's say you have a personality clash with your boss, or your boss is threatened by you, or you have a lame duck of a boss who always takes the line of least resistance and does not fight for you. As you can imagine, any one of these scenarios will hold back your advancement. Your boss, in these instances, becomes what we will call a 'Blocker' – she or he blocks your career path or your access to the executive decision-maker/s who can open that path.

If you do have a Blocker for a boss and you want to get ahead, you are going to have to make a few choices. You can either:
- go over your boss's head and perhaps irrevocably damage your relationship with her, or
- stay where you are and stop climbing, or
- change companies or departments.

But what if you are happy in your job and you don't want to make a change? What if your boss is just a big fat Blocker? First prize is to arrange to see an executive decision-maker with the support of your boss. This is not as difficult as it may sound – I'm talking about getting your boss's backing, even if your boss is Mr Lame Duck. We'll talk about the scary prospect of being in front of Mr Big boss (in referring to Mr Big, I do, of course, mean Ms Big as well) in a moment.

To win your boss's support for you to see an executive, you need to show your boss how it will be to her benefit. For example, you could say to her that you are going to set up a meeting between yourself and Mr Big because you want to tell Mr Big how helpful she has been in helping you grow within your position, and you're sure Mr Big is not aware of how she is developing her people. Did you notice that, in the example, you are not *asking* for permission to see Mr Big, you are *telling* your boss why you are *going* to see Mr Big? Whatever you do, be sincere. Find some way of showing your boss that your going to see Mr Big will not make her look bad.

Are you thinking to yourself that the example I have just used is manipulative? Well, it probably is, but is manipulation a good or a bad trait? The answer to that question is 'it depends', and what it depends upon is your motive. If your motive does no harm to anyone (beware that Wiccan curse!), then manipulation is not a bad thing

– it's just a form of extreme selling. If you are uncomfortable with manipulation, then you need to find a method with which you are comfortable that shows your boss how it will be of benefit to her for you to see Mr Big.

All this talk of being in front of the powers that be may be making you nervous and you may be quietly thinking to yourself that it is not really necessary to see Mr Big. Let me tell you again why it *is* important that Mr Big knows your name. You want to be front of mind at all levels, including the executives, when they start looking for someone to promote or to give an important project to.

Another reason. Let's say your boss wants to promote you and give you a decent increase, but the financial director of your company has said that you can have the promotion but not the increase (she is now a Blocker). How can you influence or overturn this decision? By seeing the financial director's boss. You need to know who can say 'yes' when someone else has said 'no'. If you can get in front of Finance Woman's boss and present a *Valid Business Case* on why you should get the increase, your chances of getting it are exponentially improved.

There are consequences to going over people's heads in order to see the big bosses, the most important of which is deciding whether or not this will damage your relationship with the Blocker. First prize is being able to present to the Blocker a *Valid Business Case* on how she will benefit from your meeting with Mr Big. If going over a Blocker's head will damage the relationship and you can find no way to justify this to the Blocker, you need to make a call – stay as you are and be happy at the bottom of the ladder, or take the chance and leap up the ladder two rungs at a time.

If you think this is all too pushy, that's fine, but be aware that you are being reactive and not proactive in managing your climb up the ladder. It's going to take you a lot longer to get to the top if you are putting your fate in a Blocker's hands.

BIG, SCARY BOSSES

'A good boss makes his men realise they have more ability than they think they have so that they consistently do better work than they thought they could.' – *Charles Erwin Wilson* *(American businessman and politician; 1890–1961)*

It is important to get in front of the decision-makers or the powers that be or Mr Big for one simple reason – they need to know who you are. They (this could be a person or a board of directors) hold the fate of your career in their hands. They can make your life easy or difficult. They can also be your greatest allies and your most influential mentors. Having access to Mr Big does not give *you* the power, but it sure gives you access to the power.

First things first. The big boss may seem like some kind of scary monster, and in a few isolated cases, this perception will unfortunately be true, but when you are actually face to face with a very powerful person, you will usually find someone with charm, grace, wisdom and decent people skills. Just do not waste his or her time! Dr Bruce Banner can then become the Incredible Hulk. We'll talk about what you need to do to avoid provoking the Incredible Hulk in a moment, but what's important for now is to go into the meeting expecting Bruce Banner and not the Hulk. What can you do to prepare the scaredy-cat inside you for the meeting?

Mr Big is a normal person. He gets punctures, he has sick kids, his family causes him stress, he goes to the loo. Before we go any further, let me share my own little horror story with you. When I was in my early thirties, I left the comfort of the corporate world to move full time into my own business. I had secured the local agency for Miller Heiman, then the world's leading sales-process training system, which meant that I had to go out and sell. I had never formally sold before and was pretty much petrified of calling on the executive strata of business (or 'C' level as they are called today – as in chief executive officer (CEO), chief financial officer (CFO), chief information officer (CIO), etc.). I had been taught by Miller Heiman that executives make the final buying decisions – something that has been proven correct time and time again – so I understood that this was the level at which I needed to be selling – but it didn't stop the terror.

My mentor at the time was Nick Speare, head of the European operation for Miller Heiman. Nick encouraged me to imagine the chief executives on whom I would be calling in a normal human situation. He joked that this would be something like picturing the person sitting on the loo. I, however, took Nick literally and on our first executive call, I imagined the big boss with whom I was meeting to be sitting on the loo. I was now not only terrified, but also had the giggles to control.

What Nick was saying was this: Don't deify Mr Big, because he is a human too. He will have his good and his bad days, but terror for terror's sake is not going to help you improve your confidence. Nick took the time and trouble to accompany me on my sales calls and gently taught me how to sell to the C level. It completely turned the tide in my selling career.

Some of the most charming people I have met in business have also been the most senior. Dr Michael Jordaan, CEO of First National Bank, and Tokyo Sexwale, executive chairman of the Mvelaphanda Group, spring to mind. I find the problematic ones to be the middle-management layer of business, where the players are still trying to prove themselves. They are the clever Dicks and mean bastards. This is far less common with Mr Big.

When I Googled 'advice for dealing with executives' to see if I could find anything additional on the subject, I came across lots of sites dedicated to dealing with psychotype executives. The good news is that for every one of these you may come across in business, you will meet nine fabulous people. Want to turn these nine into monsters? Waste their time. Be sure you know why you want to see Mr Big – your *Valid Business Case* – and be doubly sure of what you will say. This way, you can keep the Incredible Hulk at bay.

THE MEETING OF IMPORTANCE

'Good fortune is what happens when opportunity meets with planning.'
— *Thomas A Edison (American inventor; 1847–1931)*

Your first meeting with Mr Big will be your most critical. It's back to that damn first-impressions thing. The old saying goes, 'You only get one chance to make a first impression.' And unfortunately that's true, so you have to look the part, be the part and say the part to the very best of your abilities.

Let's assume you have successfully convinced your direct boss of the merits of your seeing Mr Big, or you have been called in by Mr Big to do a presentation or give feedback on a project. You are now master – or madam – of your own destiny, so you need to make sure that you don't screw up the opportunity. First things first: ensure that you look your best. Take time to decide on an outfit, fix your hair and do all the other impression-driven stuff. Then comes the real work. You need to plan very carefully what you are going to say and how you are going to present your case.

We'll come back to the content, but let's talk about protocol for a moment. You must decide if your presentation is going to be informal, or if you'll use slides. How will you address Mr Big – by his first name, or by his surname, or perhaps as 'Sir'? Yes, you need to drill down to this level of preparation. Where will you meet? Will it be in Mr Big's office, or will you suggest another suitable venue? Even plan your introduction. Bouncing into the office and saying, 'Hi, I'm Thandi. I just popped in to see how you are doing,' will not win you points. Saying something like, 'Good morning, Mr Big. I am Thandi Smith. I set up this meeting to present to you how I plan to increase sales in the ladies' shoes department, if I'm successful in securing the position as head of merchandising.' Now you have his attention.

By the way, did you notice that I used Thandi's surname in the second example? Any self-respecting Work Diva uses her first name *and* her surname in the corporate world – having only one name is associated with the bimbo brigade, and they tend not to do very well with the executives.

Now for content. Senior executives are busy people. They do not like their time to be wasted. One of the reasons executives employ secretaries or personal assistants is so that this people person can act as a gatekeeper (or Blocker, if you prefer) – to protect them from time-wasters. Here is a very important piece of advice: you need to have a *Valid Business Case* for seeing an executive – something valid to *them*, not you! Never ever go unprepared into a meeting with an executive. If you are called into a meeting and have had no time to prepare, present yourself at the meeting, find out what the executive wants, and then tell him or her you need time to prepare and would appreciate a date in the diary to present whatever it is that he or she wants from you. Do not try flying by the seat of your pants – it'll end in tears.

The big bosses are interested in the impact whatever it is you are planning or doing will have on the organisation – that is your *Valid Business Case*. Typically, this would be something like:
- improving the company's financial results in some way;
- increasing the company's market share;
- decreasing the company's expense base;
- beating the competition; or
- maximising a return on investment (or 'ROI' as they will call it).

The powers that be do not want to talk about operational detail. They want to discuss the strategic issues affecting the business. In order to have a meaningful discussion about these types of issues, you must do your homework. If it is market share you're going to be discussing, you will need to understand the current size of the company's market share, how this is measured, etc. Is reading *Cosmo* going to help you? Of course not, so what can you do to prepare for these high-level discussions?

Reading is good. Reading is always good – but read the *business* newspapers and magazines. Find books – even novels (any reading is better than none) – set in the business world. And if you don't understand something you read, find out what it means. Watch the business channels on television. Get coaching from someone who understands how businesses operate at the strategic level. Not only are you preparing to interface with executives, you're preparing yourself to become an executive.

If you're quite junior in an organisation, C-level people will usually be sympathetic to your efforts to learn and are likely to cut you a little slack. They will still expect you to know your subject and to have done your homework.

Back to the executive meeting. Let's use Thandi Smith as our example. Imagine Thandi works for Selfridges as an assistant merchandiser in the ladies' shoes department, and she is hoping to be promoted to head of merchandising for the department. In presenting to Mr Big, Thandi should be able to explain how placing the Jimmy Choo, Christian Louboutin, Manolo Blahnik or Patrick Cox shoes in one 'high-end' area with displays dedicated to each shoe manufacturer – sponsored by the manufacturer – will increase sales based on a pilot project she did last month.

Knowing lots about shoes will serve Thandi well, but Mr Big wants to know how the shoe displays can increase business. He is not interested in the quality or the range or the seasonal colours of the shoes. Any quality concerns, for example, would need to be raised with the quality assurance manager. Only if Sarah Ferguson had bought a pair of shoes that were poor quality and she had subsequently tripped and shown her knickers on television would Mr Big be inclined to get involved in this side of the business. Does this make sense? Mr Big needs the big picture.

How does all of this affect you? If you want to elevate your career, the people making the decisions that affect your career path need to know who you are and what capabilities you have. Who better to present this to them than you? But be sure to present it in such a way that they can see the relevance of what you are saying to the organisation as a whole. Are they interested in the fact that your boss is picking on you or pinching your bum? No – go and see human resources for that. Are they interested in a new software product you have found to increase the processor speeds in the office? No – go and see the IT manager.

What if you can't get into Mr Big's office and you know that you must see him to be considered for a big promotion? What if his secretary is the gatekeeper from hell? All you need to know is what time the gatekeeper leaves the office and, once she is gone, phone Mr Big directly. He'll probably fob you off by saying, 'Get Lucifer to put it in my dairy.' When Luci comes in the next morning, you can tell her that Mr Big wants to see you and give her a date and a time for the diary.

Only once you have gained the confidence of the powers that be should you risk talking about peripheral issues like the weather or their children or golf – unless, of course, they initiate these conversations with you. If they do, don't overstay your welcome (on the subject or in their office). While you are an unknown quantity, impress them with your preparation and understanding of the big business issues, as well as your knowledge of your specific area of the business.

TEN TIPS FOR MEETING WITH MR BIG

'People who enjoy meetings should not be in charge of anything.'
– *Thomas Sowell (American writer and economist; 1930–?)*

I found this article on www.dumblittleman.com, written for Dumb Little Man by Chrissy Scivicque, and thought it offered very useful insights into meeting with the Big Boss.

Ten tips for a successful meeting with the boss

Maybe you work one-on-one with the head honcho every day or perhaps you only get a face-to-face on the very rare occasion. Whenever you get the chance to sit down and have a meeting with the big guns, it's best to make it as productive as possible. It's also a chance to show your stuff and leave a lasting impression of who you are and what you have to offer. Here are ten ways to help you do that.

1. **Ask for an agenda prior to the meeting**
    If there's not one available, offer to create one to help keep the meeting focused and on track. If the meeting is less formal than that, be sure the goal of the meeting is at least spoken out loud and agreed upon by both of you. Knowing the goal of the meeting you can then gather any appropriate documentation you might need to take with you. For example, if the meeting is to review your performance and discuss a possible promotion,

you would want to bring copies of letters from clients complimenting you on your work, a table showing your recent sales and the impact they had on your team, etc.

2. **Dress to impress**

   Not much needs to be said about this one except that it is more important than you probably think. Even if the normal dress at your company is fairly casual, step it up a few notches. You want your boss to take notice. You should look better than you do on a regular basis.

3. **Take notes during the meeting**

   This shows that you are listening and that you plan to review what was discussed later. It also indicates that you are already considering the follow-up that will be done after the meeting. The notes are handy for exactly this reason. You may come out of the meeting with a list of action items that you will need to remember to take care of in the future.

4. **Show enthusiasm and positivity**

   Plain and simple. Just like you do for a job interview, put on the shiny-happy hat. Yes, it's true that sometimes you have to address a complaint, and in that case see number 5 ...

5. **Bring solutions**

   Never enter a meeting with a complaint that you don't have at least one solution for. I know this is difficult but how are you going to enter a meeting with your boss, hand him a problem and then say 'you work it out'? He's going to throw it right back to you and ask what you think the answer is. Go in prepared. In my opinion, you should take two or three possible solutions. If you are absolutely stuck, you must express that you've given the topic much consideration and ruled out several possible solutions in the process. At least then you've shown the effort.

6. Build rapport

Make a connection with your boss. This is going to vary for every situation but try to show a little personality. Most people in a leadership position have great social personalities. You just have to coax it out of them sometimes. If you know their favourite ball team, comment on how they've been doing. If you know they play golf, ask how their game is doing. If they like jazz, tell them about a new jazz band you heard recently. Do your research and be prepared for a little small talk.

7. Show vision

Don't be afraid to voice big ideas. Show your understanding (or curiosity) for the bigger picture. Don't limit yourself by sticking to topics related only to your job. Show broad interest and they'll start looking at you as a potential future leader.

8. Ask clarification questions

Don't ever – and I mean EVER – say that you understand something if you don't. I can't stress this enough. Remember the episode of *Seinfeld* when George is working on a project for his boss and he has no idea what it is? George didn't hear his boss, but acted like he understood the assignment. Next thing he knew, he was in charge of something that was a complete mystery. Excellent episode. But also very apt. People always nod and go along with things in a meeting thinking that they can figure it out later. Don't leave that office with questions. I have learned that the hard way. So now, I ask questions and then, before I leave, I restate what we've discussed and accomplished.

9. Send thanks

Either by e-mail, mail or with a telephone call, let your boss know you appreciate the time he spends with you. Whatever is most appropriate. I see my boss every day and meet with him every day, but if we have a special one-on-one, I make sure to say thank you at the end of the day to reinforce that I know it was out of the ordinary and I appreciate the time.

10. Follow up

If you leave with a list of action items, try to establish agreed-upon dates when they should be accomplished. Then, follow through and meet that deadline. I used to work with someone who talked big during meetings and then never followed through. So meetings became pointless. Don't let this happen and think your boss won't notice. He'll notice. He might not approach the topic, but he'll notice.

WHEN THE EXECUTIVES HAVE THEIR SAY

'Authority without wisdom is like a heavy axe without an edge, fitter to bruise than polish.'
— *Anne Bradstreet*
(American writer and poet; c. 1612–1672)

As part of my research for this book I interviewed, formally and informally, several highly regarded men and women holding executive positions. I posed a variety of questions to them, but what I basically wanted to know was, 'What does a Work Diva need to do to ensure her success in the corporate world?' Here is invaluable input from two of South Africa's leading business lights.

Dr Michael Jordaan is chief executive officer (CEO) of First National Bank, one of the four biggest commercial banks in South Africa. Although I hardly know Michael, he was kind enough to find time in his diary (though let me tell you, I had to work very hard on my *Valid Business Case* to get the appointment) and equally generous with his views.

I was so pleased to get the appointment that I neglected part of my preparation for the meeting. I planned my questions, I planned how to get to the venue, what I would wear and so on, but I forgot to check Michael's current business profile. So, when I asked him during our meeting how far his span of control stretched, he looked at me a little blankly and said, 'I run the bank?' Luckily for me, Michael is renowned for his impeccable manners, intelligence, charm and modesty.

Michael considers himself to be a humanist and, as such, does not subscribe to any form of prejudice – he emphasised that the input he was giving was directed at males and females. Michael also believes that women have the right to choose to work.

The key pointers Michael shares here – based on his experience of the international and local business environments – will benefit would-be Work Divas everywhere:

– Women should be doing better in business but are held back because of prejudices and stereotypes. We need to get rid of the biases while making allowances for the differences between people.

– To overcome these prejudices and stereotypes, women need to focus on their own development, particularly education and training.

– People who make the most effort will rise to the top, regardless of the unfairness they may face.

– Make use of mentors – this is particularly important for people who come from a base of disadvantage.

– Men are ego-driven, whereas women don't let ego get in the way. Men and women need to be sensitive to what drives the other sex.

Michael closed off by saying, 'Understand that you can get support from everywhere, so making the most of your life and your career is up to you. Take ownership and you will be more successful. Empowerment is so much more powerful when you empower yourself.'

Brenda Bensted-Smith is CEO of Ad Talent, South Africa's premiere advertising and marketing recruitment company. More than that, Brenda is one of the most generous and vivacious women I have ever had the pleasure of meeting, in both my business and personal lives. It is interesting that Brenda judges her own success by how many other people she has made successful.

Here are Brenda's practical guidelines for overcoming, and making the most of, being a woman in a male-dominated world:

- Because they relate quicker to one another, women can be relaxed with each other, but should be more professional when dealing with men.
- Giving off a vibe that you are 'available' can lead to an unwelcome pass. If you are not available, signal this very clearly to the men you deal with and you will, in most cases, avoid the pinched bum.
- Part of the vibe you give off is in how you dress – dress like a professional and you will be treated with professionalism. If you are unsure of how to dress, get advice.
- The more confident you appear and look, the better it will serve you.
- Always be prepared. If you are unprepared – for a meeting, a presentation, whatever – you will not be taken seriously. Know your subject and your industry intimately.

Brenda believes that women need to be more assertive when dealing with men than when interacting with other women. This, she says, is because women find it easy to establish personal bonds, whereas they can't rely on these bonds when interfacing with men.

The opportunity to obtain insight from two outstanding business leaders, people who actually live what they say, is rare. Take this advice to heart, dear diva, and you, too, will be able to breathe the thin air at the very top of the ladder.

Chapter 10

RUNG 7:
WHEN SEX REARS ITS HEAD

THE BATTLE OF SEX

> 'Nobody will ever win the Battle of the Sexes. There's just too much fraternising with the enemy.'
> — *Henry Kissinger*
> *(American diplomat and Nobel Peace Prize laureate; 1923–?)*

What does 'the battle of the sexes' really mean? Is it any competition between males and females, or is it limited to the business context? Could it be that both sexes want more or less the same thing, but use very different methods to achieve success? I'm not sure that these questions are even the right ones to be asking, but is it not time to move away from the stereotypical nonsense and accept that maybe it's really about the sex battle between the sexes?

There are lots of well-intentioned pressure groups trying to bring about equality between men and women. I am one hundred per cent behind the organisations that fight for equal opportunities, equal pay, equal everything, but they lose me when they try to make us the same. Why do they lament the differences between men and women instead of celebrating them?

Vive la différence! Being different does, of course, mean that conflict is bound to arise, and none more so than in the way in which men and women approach sex in the workplace. Women are accused of using sex to sell; men are accused of being sexual predators. Men accuse women of using sex to get ahead; women point fingers back at the men for being part of the plot. Where does it start and end? I have no idea, but I do think that we need to have a little dig around to see what we can find. There are frivolous and serious sides to the sex-in-business coin, and we will explore both.

Karen Salmansohn, author of the delightfully titled book *How to Succeed in Business without a Penis*, writes wittily on the sex battle between men and women. Ms Salmansohn remarks:

> *Women must learn to go that extra distance to stand out in the competitive career marketplace. It's hard enough to succeed in business with a penis these days ... A woman doesn't need a penis to succeed in business. Though she does need balls. Also, a good set of boobs doesn't hurt either. Basically, every business-woman needs to learn how to juggle all four entities: balls and boobs.*

One of my abiding memories of sex and business is a story my larger-than-life friend, Patrick the Redhead, shared with me. Patrick told me that an ex-boss of his, whom I also happened to know, had told Patrick that one should always recruit sales people with a high sex drive, as it is directly linked to business drive, and those with a high sex drive achieve better results than people with a low sex drive.

How the boss determined sex drive in the interview process I have yet to establish, but it does afford some interesting speculation! I am still trying to prove or disprove this theory – without getting myself into trouble – and when I find the answer, I'll write a book about it. In the meantime, let's take a gentle look at the role sex plays in the business environment and how it can help or hamper the Work Diva's climb up the corporate ladder.

WILY WOMEN AND FOXY DIVAS

> 'The thing women have got to learn is that nobody gives you power.
> You just take it.'
>   – *Roseanne Barr*
> *(American comedian and actor; 1952–?)*

A few times now I have referred to feminine wiles, and always in a positive manner. What are feminine wiles? How should the Work Diva use them? When are they not appropriate? How do they fit into the male vs female dynamic?

Let's start with the definition of 'feminine wiles'. Do you know that I could not find one formal definition of feminine wiles? This does give the Work Divas a wonderful opportunity – we'll make up our very own definition. 'Feminine' is defined by www.yourdictionary.com as 'having qualities regarded as characteristic of women and girls, as gentleness, weakness, delicacy, or modesty'. Weakness? Not feckin' likely. What if we define 'feminine' as 'the art of being a strong woman, using grace, charm and intelligence'? 'Wiles', as associated with foxes, is commonly defined as 'a trick or cunning ruse'. How, then, does 'foxy' get to mean 'One hot spunky piece of ass', according to www.urbandictionary.com? I think our 'wiles' should be 'smart, sassy and cunning', don't you?

This leaves us with the following definition: 'feminine wiles – a strong woman who uses her grace and charm to get what she wants in a smart, sassy manner'. Like that? If not, feel free to write your own definition. Go for it – there's nobody out there telling us what it should be!

Using our very own definition, how do feminine wiles fit into the male-dominated business world? Early on in *Work Diva* I listed the fact of women having feminine wiles as being a good thing. I suggested that women are generally more intuitive, cunning and manipulative than men, yet most don't trust or use their feminine wiles. I went on to say that in an environment where chauvinists – who are susceptible to feminine wiles – abound, women should use these talents. Where does one draw the line?

I found an article written by Maureen Sanders, president of High Road Solutions, which said that, in the context of feminine wiles, it's not really that difficult to determine what behaviour is acceptable and what is not. As long as a woman is not trading her sexuality for recognition, promotion, increases, etc., she is fine. Ms Sanders goes on to say that an attractive woman need not play down her beauty in order to maintain professional legitimacy, because what makes people attractive is their self-assurance. She believes that when a woman is confident in herself and her ability, she does not need to resort to flashing a bit more leg or cleavage. Fair comment, but who said feminine wiles were about the physical and sexual? What about the mental? Women are more than 'pieces of ass'.

Feminine wiles are a woman's ability to use the power of suggestion, to be sassy and smart, in getting what she wants. Does this bring us back to manipulation? Perhaps, but, as I have said before, manipulation is not necessarily a bad thing. So, maybe using feminine wiles is a woman getting what she wants through her own intelligent, sassy brand of manipulation. I like it!

You've no doubt heard the old saying that goes, 'If you've got it, flaunt it.' I am not blessed in the boob department, so I've never taken this out for a run – although I do understand that the saying extends beyond the chest. Perhaps the 'flaunt it' is that fine line. Contrary to Ms Sanders, I think a flash of leg or a little cleavage is okay, even enticing, but, for heaven's sake, don't show too much! I was calling on the country managing director of a large IT company recently and was greeted by a huge pair of boobs, with the nipples squeezing out to say hello too. I was embarrassed by all the flesh on display – and I'm a woman! What on earth did the male visitors think? Was the receptionist touting for a part in a blue movie? I discreetly pulled the managing director's secretary aside and suggested that she speak to Ms Porn Star at the front desk about basic business decorum.

Being sassy and a little foxy is fabulous. Using your feminine wiles is making use of a talent that only us girls have, and any advantage we can get that doesn't violate our personal values, we should take!

THE S.E.X. FACTOR

'I knew when I walked into the lunchroom and my boss was reading
Hustler, it was going to be bad.'   – *Edith Magee*
(American labourer and sexual harassment claimant)

We have already touched lightly on the subject of unwelcome overtures, but what
happens when S.E.X. does raise its head, so to speak? What's a diva to do? Sexual
passes can, of course, be welcome or unwelcome, but let's deal with the welcome
ones for the moment.

Four out of every ten people meet their spouse at the office, says a very interesting article by Coulson Duerksen that I found at www.health.discovery.com. I met
my man at work, and, if I look around at my friends, more than four in ten of them
seem to have met their partners through business. Considering that work consumes
such a huge chunk of our waking hours, it's no surprise that this is such a popular
mate-hunting ground.

Talking about the *welcome* overtures, if you meet a man in the office and he is
single, then there should be no issue, right? But what is 'single'? Is a man in a long-
term relationship single? Is an unhappily married man single? You need to draw your
own line as to what is fair game and what is off-limits. The women I know who
have had relationships with married men – even when the man leaves his wife –
have usually ended up miserable and alone. Now that I'm thinking about it, only
one of my friends who found herself involved with a married man has enjoyed a
happy ending to her story. The scandal and drama affairs create in the office mean
that you need to think very carefully about your choices, especially if you are serious
about your career.

Back to single men in the office. These relationships still create gossip, so be prepared for some unpleasantness, regardless of whom you are having a relationship
with. Office affairs create tensions, especially if they are with the boss. So, should
you sleep with the boss, bearing in mind we are talking about welcome passes?

Here are three serious consequences for you to consider before you leap between the bed sheets with the boss:

1. Is he married or involved? Even if he tells you that he is desperately unhappy – and he might well be – *you* will be seen as the scarlet woman and your work record will be tarnished for a very long time to come. Don't do the married men, boss or not, and you will save yourself a lot of heartache in the long run.

2. If you are promoted, your promotion will be viewed with suspicion – was she promoted because she slept with the boss? While this may or may not be true, it will damage your career – now and in the future. The business community is not as big as you think. Sleeping with the boss *always* has a price. If you don't pay it now, you will pay for it later in your career. Do you really want to climb the ladder bed by bed, rather than on your own merits and hard work? If you fall in love with your boss, leave the company. That way, you will always be beyond reproach.

3. What happens when it all goes wrong? Sorry, sister, but you'll be leaving the company sooner than you can imagine. You can try to wave the sexual harassment stick, but the courts are not terribly sympathetic to women who sleep with the boss and then expect a supportive shoulder.

If it's not the boss and you do decide to embark on a relationship with someone in the office, there are still a few things for you to consider. Is it against company policy? What if you have an ugly break-up – who stays and who goes? What if he is not discreet, and the innermost details of your performance end up on the company's intranet? How do you save face if you get dumped? How do you dump him without rubbing his nose in it every day? What if you find out that you have a competitor in the office?

There are a lot of 'whats' and 'ifs' to consider, but in reality you still have a pretty good chance of finding happiness in the office. Just use your judgement, dear diva.

THE ON AND OFF OF OFFICE ROMANCES

'Affairs are easier of entrance than of exit; and it is but common prudence to see our way out before we venture in.'
  – Aesop (Ancient Greek slave and storyteller; 620–560 BC)

You will find many interesting, and conflicting, articles about office affairs on the internet, in magazines and in books. Should you embark on an office romance, or shouldn't you? In reality, most of us will become romantically involved with a colleague at some point in our careers. This comes down to statistics as much as it does to love. Maybe this is a cynical point of view, but think about it – how much time do you spend at the office? How much time do you spend in cocktail bars or at parties? Surely the chances of meeting a lover are proportionate to the amount of time you spend in a place where love could cross your path?

Here are seven dos and don'ts, pros and cons, to consider if you are thinking about pursuing, or are involved in, an office romance:

1. Married or not?

If either of you is married, your office relationship will be fraught with problems. Your colleagues are going to speculate and gossip, no matter how discreet you try to be. The Work Diva of substance tells the truth, remember, whatever the consequences. The Work Diva of substance keeps her promises – and marriage vows are promises. If you are not able to tell the truth or keep your promises, should you be doing what you are doing? If you fall in love and you are married, get divorced and then pursue your relationship. Or change your marriage arrangement to one of an open relationship. 'It's not that easy, there are children to consider,' you might say. If that is the case, then think very carefully about your extramarital behaviour. Will having an affair not lead to a breakdown in the marriage anyway? Has your marriage not already broken down if you are having affairs?

2. Sleeping with the boss

We've already looked at the consequences of having sex with the boss. Recast your eye over the point above. Married? *Don't.* Discreet? *Forget it* – there will be even more speculation and gossip if the boss man is involved. If you are single and your boss is single and you are prepared to move companies if need be, go for it. Be aware, though, that problems will *still* surface. Others in the workplace may be jealous of your relationship; any promotions or salary increases you receive will be viewed with suspicion; his colleagues may be concerned about pillow talk. It's a dangerous game, so play it only if you are prepared for the fallout.

3. To tell or not to tell

In both of the points above I have mentioned gossip. The quickest and easiest way to stop the gossip? Be open and honest about your relationship. The sooner it is out in the public domain, the sooner all the glances and giggles directed at the two of you will stop. If you have something to hide, should you be having the relationship at all? The interesting thing about office affairs is that the other people in the office seem to think that they have a 'right' to know about them – it's almost as if the relationship belongs to the company. Honesty is hugely disarming, so use it to protect your love affair.

4. It's a matter of trust

Many years ago I worked with a very competitive man who took great delight in discussing with his male colleagues the most personal details of his romantic conquests. Owing to the fact that I was dating one of his colleagues at the time, I too got to hear all the saucy details. When he had bedded someone in the office, the whole company soon knew what she looked like without her clothes, the sexiness (or not) of her underwear, how 'good she was in the sack on a scale of one to ten', and even specifics about the most intimate of acts that they had performed. All I can say is, thank goodness there was no internet in those days! Choose your affairs with caution. If he tells you all about his last love, he's sure to do the same about you if the two of you split up.

5. The office mattress

Consider *your* work environment for a moment. Can you name the women (and men) who sleep around? Of course you can. The water-cooler conversations ensure that you are kept informed of all the bed-hopping that goes on in your office. There is a saying in showbiz that any publicity is better than no publicity. Are you sure that you want to become 'famous' in your office for all the wrong reasons? If you are serious about your career, it's best not to get branded as the office mattress. It may make you popular, but not for reasons that will help you to rise to the top of the organisation, so to speak.

6. The end of the affair

Who stays and who goes when it all blows up? If you were having an affair with your boss, *you* are the one who gets to look for a new job, like it or not. If it's a colleague whom you'll see regularly afterwards, a split can make for sad and difficult times. You may already have experienced the pain of having to encounter someone you love, but who does not feel the same way about you, on a daily basis. In the office environment, hysterical scenes and breakdowns are simply not acceptable. You must control your haywire emotions and behave with as much dignity as possible. This is especially difficult if you get dumped for someone else in the office – ouch! But what if you ended it? How do you avoid rubbing his nose in it every day? What if he is bad-mouthing you? Well, the same applies. You need to control your emotions, and your mouth, and try to lift yourself above the ugliness that so often accompanies the break-up of a relationship. It may be easier, ultimately, to find a new job.

7. Company policy and corporate police

This is probably the least interesting – or is that the least juicy? – of all the issues relating to office romances, but it is one of the most important. Why do some companies prohibit their staff from having affairs in the workplace? There are lots of good reasons, according to the corporate police: Office romances may negatively impact productivity and morale, they can introduce time-wasting gossip and politics into the organisation, people could be hired, fired or promoted for the wrong reasons, potential sexual harassment claims and breaches of corporate governance can occur, and so on. They have a point.

So, before you embark on an office affair, have a close look at how it will impact your career. After all, you are trying to climb the corporate ladder, not get thrown off it!

HARASSMENT AND OTHER HORRORS

'Sexual harassment is complex, subtle, and highly subjective.'
– *Kathie Lee Gifford (American television host; 1953–?)*

While welcome overtures can bring fun, happiness and potential trouble, what about the *unwelcome* passes? Many women have had their career wrecked by sexual harassment, even if formal processes were not pursued. Women change jobs they love just to get away from wandering hands, they are subjected to soul-destroying sexual harassment cases, they are accused of unspeakable behaviour despite often being completely without blame. Women always seem to get damaged, in some shape or form, by sexual harassment cases.

There are, however, lots of instances where the woman's conduct is not whiter than white. If you are, or have been, on the receiving end of some unwanted sexual attention in the office, take a long, hard look at your own behaviour. Did you in any way give a sign that you were available? Did the way you dress send off smoke signals without your knowledge? As I said before, your clothes talk about you behind your back, so you owe it to yourself to find out what your clothes are saying. Do you have a reputation for being the office mattress?

Why I ask all these questions is because women sometimes give off signals, even unintentionally, that some poor unsuspecting man – and we are undoubtedly the smarter sex, especially when it comes to sex – may have misinterpreted. If you have even the slightest of doubts about your behaviour, you owe it to yourself, and to the man involved, to sit him down and explain that you are not interested. If he persists, then maybe you need to take further action.

A couple of my girlfriends are incredibly beautiful – and I mean drop-dead gorgeous. What's interesting is that they do get solicited more than most other women, but this is usually done in an open and direct way. They do not seem to have more sleazy approaches than any other women I know, which leads me to believe that a woman can control the wandering-hands syndrome to a large extent through her own signals and behaviour.

If you know, for absolute certain, that you did not give the 'come-on' in any way, then you need to take steps to protect yourself. I would still sit the person down – it's not always a man – and tell them that you do not appreciate the advances and that they must stop immediately, or you will be forced to take the issue further. A private discussion gives the man (back to the stereotype) the opportunity to save face, and you may well be able to stop him in his tracks. As soon as you pull in another party, regardless of who this might be, the man will be receiving a public reprimand and will feel the need to defend himself (remember what Dr Michael Jordaan said about ego) – usually by levelling accusations against you. While you might be completely and utterly innocent, this type of ugly scene is emotionally draining and can ultimately be psychologically damaging.

If the private meeting does not stop the unwelcome advances, do not hesitate to pull in professional assistance. If it was me, I would make my boss aware that I was going to approach, say, human resources, as I would want as much support from my boss as possible, and then I would approach the appropriate officer. If you do not trust your boss to support you – or if your boss is the problem – go directly to the correct channel using the correct protocol. Do not make any wrong moves.

I can hear you saying, 'But what if I'm not in the wrong? Why do *I* have to be the one being careful?' Because you do not want to damage your case – you must keep your side of the conflict as clean as possible. The person against whom you press sexual harassment charges will, in all likelihood, make counter-allegations about you. He will accuse you of behaving like a whore, dressing like a tart, making the move on him and much, much worse. Prepare yourself for an extremely unpleasant time, because, even though you may not be in any way to blame, your life is going to go through a very difficult period.

Most big companies nowadays have formal sexual harassment procedures. If your company's procedures conflict with what I have recommended here, please follow your company's process and not my suggestions.

I just want to make a plea on behalf of all the women in the working world who are trying to get ahead in business: If you are using sexual harassment charges as your personal sword of vengeance, please stop immediately. By levelling accusations of sexual harassment against all and sundry in order to correct whatever ills you believe yourself to be the victim of, you are doing the rest of us no favours. If women stopped crying wolf in rape charges and sexual harassment cases, the courts would be on our side, instead of making us defend our innocence. If you know in your heart that you are using the threat of charging someone with sexual harassment to get what you want, what you really need is professional counselling. Please get it, for the sake of all the innocent women who are sexually assaulted and harassed every day.

DRINK ME, DRINK ME!

> 'A horrid alcoholic explosion scatters all my good intentions like bits of limbs and clothes over the doorsteps and into the saloon bars of the tawdriest pubs.'
> — *Dylan Thomas*
> *(Welsh poet, author and playwright; 1914–1953)*

What is the relationship between office affairs and alcohol? I think we all know the answer to *that* question. Alcohol is undoubtedly a social lubricant. As the infamous Marquis de Sade (*French aristocrat; 1740–1814*) said, 'Conversation, like certain portions of the anatomy, always runs more smoothly when lubricated.'

My husband and I have a little ritual called 'dressing drinks'. He started it. Whenever we have to go to a function that neither of us wants to attend, we each have a double shot of tequila, with salt and lemon, of course, and off we go. We invariably have a wonderful time, but tequila is a slippery slope, so beware of adopting this tradition if you're not used to extreme alcohol.

You need to decide on your own limits, but there is nothing sadder than a drunken woman lurching around. For some reason it looks marginally less trashy when a man is drunk, but there you have it. Women need to be careful with alcohol, because the rules of intoxication are different for men and women. If you drink too much in front of the powers that be, even once, you can damage your career. The same rule does not apply to the men. The Work Diva understands this, and thus watches her intake at business functions.

I have lots of drinking buddies and we all enjoy a good night out, but we only push the envelope when we're in safe company – which, come to think about it, is quite often. I'm careful not to drink too much in front of anyone who could influence my career, but from time to time I make mistakes. The problem is that not only do I regret it the next morning – I beat myself up for weeks afterwards. 'Then why do you do it?' I hear you asking. Simple. French champagne and tequila are amongst my favourite food groups.

The British National Health Service (NHS) has a useful 'calculator' with which you can check the limits for your drinks. See http://www.units.nhs.uk/unitCalculator. html). According to the NHS, one 125-ml glass of champagne is equal to 1.75 units per day, and women are advised not to drink more than two to three units per day. This means we can have a glass or two of champagne per day. I'm sure you're not allowed to store them all up and have twenty-one units every Saturday night!

When you have a look at the list of famous people who died either from the effects of excessive alcohol or alcohol poisoning, it is a good reason to keep your alcohol intake under control. The people who have thrown their lives away on alcohol include (extracted from www.listafterlist.com, with date of death):

Dylan Thomas – 9 November 1953, writer
John Barrymore – 29 May 1942, actor
George Best – 25 November 2005, football player
Richard Burton – 5 August 1984, actor
Truman Capote – 25 August 1984, writer
Peter Cook – 9 January 1995, comedian
F Scott Fitzgerald – 21 December 1940, writer
Errol Flynn – 14 October 1959, actor
Ernest Hemingway – 2 July 1961, writer
Billie Holiday – 17 July 1959, singer
Jack Kerouac – 21 October 1969, writer
Jackson Pollock – 11 August 1956, artist
Oliver Reed – 2 May 1999, actor
Hank Williams – 1 January 1953, musician
Townes Van Zandt – 1 January 1997, musician
WC Fields – 25 December 1946, actor

A valuable article on how alcohol negatively impacts the workplace can be found on http://www.ias.org.uk/resources/factsheets/workplace.pdf. If you think you may have a problem with alcohol, don't ask your mates; be brave and take yourself off for a session at Alcoholics Anonymous (ask Google for your closest centre). Why throw your life away on alcohol?

Chapter **11**

RUNG 8:
FIVE WAYS TO FECK UP YOUR CAREER

1: BRING YOUR BAGGAGE TO WORK

> 'The professional must learn to be moved and touched emotionally,
> yet at the same time stand back objectively: I've seen a lot of damage
> done by tea and sympathy.'   – *Anthony Storr*
> *(British psychiatrist; 1920–2001)*

One of the biggest puzzlements men have with women is the range of their emotions. Women can laugh, cry, shout and smile – all in the space of one conversation. Women who are low reactors, like myself, also find these emotional scales perplexing. It is mostly, though not exclusively, women who express high degrees of emotion. If you are a very emotional person, good for you, but there is a time and place for emotional outpourings, and I'm afraid the work environment is not one of them.

Let's put this in context. As I have said before, we are all just perfect as we are, but sometimes our behaviour needs to be modified in order for us to be able to maximise situations or integrate comfortably into relationships. With relationships, I am referring to families, spouses, co-workers, bosses, friends, strangers and the like. Many women are unable to separate themselves from their emotions, and thus permanently carry with them all their hurt, anger, bitterness, sorrow, anxiety, elation, exuberance, etc. Every single one of us has emotional scars, but what determines if we are well balanced or not is whether we are controlled by our emotions, or are in control of our emotions. When you are not able to separate yourself from states of extreme emotion, you are automatically sharing your emotional baggage with the people you encounter, whether you like it or not.

The Work Diva takes only her Lulu Guinness or Anya Hindmarch with her to the office. She leaves, as best she can, her emotional baggage at home. Why is this important? Because to succeed in the work environment you need to present only the very best of you at the office. The work space is a very competitive place. There are huge crowds at the bottom of the ladder, all looking to climb to the top. If you want to distinguish yourself from the masses, being the ultimate 'you' is the best way to do it. But how, I hear you ask, can I leave my emotional baggage behind?

It is not an easy task to separate your emotions from your self, because you are, to a large extent, made up of those very emotions. The happy news is that I've devised a relatively simple four-step exercise, which I've called the 'Emotion Action Plan', to help you achieve this seemingly difficult goal. I say 'relatively' simple because the process is uncomplicated, but it does require a fair amount of soul-searching on your part. Here we go:

Step 1

You will need to use a worksheet like the one at the end of these steps. In the left-hand column, under the title 'Extreme Emotions', write a list of all the intense emotions you feel that you believe *do not serve you* – the ones that get you into trouble, or that people you respect suggest you should control, or those emotions that make you feel uncomfortable and miserable. Bear in mind that we are looking for Extreme Emotions, not a list of everything you feel. And it's okay to put PMS on the list if it causes you to become a raving lunatic once a month. Take your time to identify all your manic emotions, as identification is the backbone of the whole exercise.

Step 2

Next – and this will probably take the most time – in the middle column next to the Extreme Emotion, write down what you believe to be the 'Root Cause' of that emotion. This may require you to sit quietly and dig deep into your past to find the original trigger for that emotion. Let's say you have 'anger' as an Extreme Emotion, and next to it you write, 'husband's affair with X' as the Root Cause. Take a moment to explore if this really is the cause, or if your anger perhaps stems from your father abandoning your mother when you were young. It's okay if you have anger, or any emotion, listed more than once if you believe you have several Root Causes for that emotion. Again, take your time. If this part of the exercise takes you two months, so be it.

Step 3

In the last column, write down *all* the ideas you have to 'Deal with it' for every emotion. For example, you might write down 'forgive' next to the Root Cause (which is your husband's affair) of your Extreme Emotion (which is anger). Do not skimp on the details. If, like me, you're not sure you understand what forgiveness really means, then say, 'Forgive and get coaching in forgiveness from Y,' providing Y is someone you believe understands forgiveness. It could be a friend, a spiritual leader, or someone you trust and respect.

If the 'Deal with it' for dealing with your husband's infidelity is to have an affair with someone yourself, then write it down. Do not judge your thoughts at this stage – that comes later. Just dump down what you think are the best ways for *you* to deal with the Root Cause of each Extreme Emotion. You need to be very honest with yourself. If you just write stuff on the list to get the exercise over and done with, then I strongly suggest you rather skip doing it. This is your life we're talking about, and it deserves a proper investment.

Step 4

Go through each Deal-with-it idea and sort the good ones from the bad, scratching the bad ones off the list. What's bad? The ones that will get you into trouble with your family or friends, spouse or employer, the law or whoever. Once you've done that, you now have an Emotion Action Plan that is going to help you reclaim your life from the manic emotions that are pulling your strings. Keep checking your progress against your list, and the day you tick off your last item, have a ceremonial burning of the list, because you will finally be freed from your demons.

The best *you* needs to present herself at work every day if you are going to become a real Work Diva. Enjoy your emotions, wallow in your emotions, savour them even, but recognise when they are damaging and controlling you. Take back the control, diva.

EMOTION ACTION PLAN		
Extreme Emotion	**Root Cause**	**Deal-with-it strategy**
(e.g.) Anger	John's affair with Jill	1. Forgive John; get coaching on this from Jack 2. Have affair with Jacob
(e.g.) Grief	Dad leaving Mom	Get professional counselling
(e.g.) PMS	Hormones?	1. Fire gynae and get new one 2. Consult an endocrinologist

2: SELL OUT ON SECRETS

'The vanity of being known to be trusted with a secret is generally one of the chief motives to disclose it.' — *Samuel Johnson* *(English author and compiler of the first dictionary; 1709–1784)*

There are people whom you can trust with your secrets, and then there are those you know for sure will not keep your confidences. Which of the two are you? We can't all be great keepers of confidences, because we know that there are those who disclose secrets. People have died under torture to keep secrets, others have simply taken their silence with them to their graves. Others are happy to sell secrets, and some just give them away for free.

If you know you are not able to keep a confidence, then, if possible, *before* someone tells you a secret, let that person know that you are hopeless at keeping them. If they still tell you, fine, that is their decision. Don't pretend you can keep a confidence if you can't – that is just deceitful. As the American actor and author Will Rogers said, 'Letting the cat out the bag is a whole lot easier than putting it back.' You should, though, be able to pride yourself on your ability to keep confidences. Being able to respect confidentiality helps you to develop a reputation for being someone others can trust.

Certain people attract other people's secrets. I have a friend, Belinda Masselli, who is a secret-magnet. She does not ask to be told everyone's secrets; people just offload their secrets on her. I think it is Belinda's serenity and warmth that draw people to her, but even those she doesn't know well will tell her their secrets. I'm not sure I would want that kind of responsibility, but I know she knows some really juicy stuff, and she just won't tell. So frustrating, but so admirable!

Why is this on the list of ways for a Work Diva to screw up her career? In business you will be exposed to a lot of confidential information. Depending on your position, this will range from information on who's about to be hired or fired, to classified business strategies and inventions. If you let a secret slip even once, you will irreparably damage your career in that company. And don't think you won't be found out.

A company I worked for many years ago was having problems with information leakage, and as head of human resources at the time, I was tasked by the managing director to out the culprit. We set traps, starting with our own board, and had to go no further. One of our directors, a charming but garrulous man, was the source of the leak. He was sharing confidential information with his secretary, who, in turn, was sharing it with all and sundry. While the director did not lose his job, he did lose the confidence of Mr Big.

If you are ever in the invidious position of being told, in confidence, by someone about something they have done that damages your organisation or even the life of another person, you need to tread very carefully. When people feel guilty about something, they often have an overwhelming desire to relieve their guilt by 'unburdening' on someone else. This can mean that you become the unlucky recipient of a terrible secret. Do you keep it or not? Do you betray the person who has told you the secret and perhaps save or protect somebody else, or do you keep the secret and watch the damage unfold before your eyes?

It is awful to have to make these types of decisions. All I can say to you, dear diva, is that you have to use your judgement. You can't even get advice on what to do without revealing the secret, so it is a lonely and difficult path. As Peter Parker's Uncle Ben said to him in *Spider-Man*, 'With great power comes great responsibility.' Well, with great secrets come great burdens.

3: BELIEVE YOUR OWN LIES

'Whether you think you can, or that you can't, you are usually right.'
– *Henry Ford (American industrialist; 1863–1947)*

Most of us believe that there is some skill or ability or talent that we were not given when we were born. 'I can't sing' (Karen and me), 'I have no physical coordination' (Julie, my tireless business director), 'I'm no good with numbers' (Nicola, Ronel). Read the quote at the top of this section. Do you know what it means? Whatever you tell yourself you can or cannot do, you then can or can't do it.

Before 6 May 1954, mankind truly believed that it was impossible to run a sub-four-minute mile. Roger Bannister believed it was possible, even though he had a life-threatening bone disease. Lance Armstrong overcame testicular cancer to become the seven-times winner of the Tour de France cycle race. In 1981, Morris Goodman, aka the Miracle Man, was told by doctors that he would never walk or be able to use any part of his body again. Eight months later, he walked out of hospital – unassisted!

There is a wonderful quote by Marianne Williamson from her book *Return to Love* (widely misattributed to Nelson Mandela and his 1994 inauguration speech), which puts into perspective the power each one of us has within. Here is an extract:

> *Our deepest fear is not that we are inadequate. Our deepest fear is that we are powerful beyond measure. It is our light, not our darkness, that most frightens us. We ask ourselves, who am I to be brilliant, gorgeous, talented, and fabulous? Actually, who are you not to be?*

If you are interested in exploring your inner power, a good place to start is with the movie *The Secret* based on the book by Rhonda Byrne. Whether you like *The Secret* or not, the message about the law of attraction is compelling.

Back to our current reality. We are what we believe – what you believe about yourself becomes your truth. Here are twelve, slightly tongue-in-cheek, classic lies we tend to tell ourselves. Which one or two apply to you?

1. I can't say no

You tell yourself you can't say no and then end up under a burden of work or other commitments with which you can't cope. You then inevitably let people down because you have taken on more than you can handle. This is a sure way to damage your career. Perhaps the truth is that you secretly pride yourself on not saying no, and take people giving you tasks or asking you for favours as a sign of their approval. Mostly they are just whipping the willing horse.

If you want to earn the respect of those around you, find a gentle way of saying no. Your fair-weather friends will soon be revealed. Start by setting yourself a few boundaries. Decide on a couple of things that you want to stop saying yes to, and then actually practise saying no. Once you get the hang of those, expand your boundaries to include the items you have more difficulty in rejecting. When you are able to start delegating, or redirecting, you're more or less cured. Also, try to find approval from those who really matter, in a more self-affirming way. Perhaps you could ask people you trust and respect to let you know when you are being assertive in a good way, or when you are standing up for yourself in a firm yet considerate manner.

2. I'm no good with numbers

This is the most common bleat I hear from women on the courses we deliver. As soon as they have a case simulation involving numbers, their minds go blank. If you are running around the office with a sign that says 'I Don't Do Numbers' on your head, you're never going to be given the important or challenging assignments that will help get you promoted.

I suspect that this aversion to numbers stems from an outdated education system many of us went through, where the boys were told they were good at the sciences and the girls were told they were good with languages and creative subjects. Here's the rub: language and mathematics are both left-brain abilities, so if you are good with languages, by definition you are good at maths, too. You probably have a mental block, not a lack of ability.

For a bit of fun, go to www.quirkology.com (it's a great site), choose the UK icon, click on 'Experiments and Tests' and then on 'Analyse Yourself', and go down to 'Test 3 – The Thumb Test'. Do the exercise. The test tells me I am right-brained, but I have always told myself I am left-brained, so, as a result, logic is one of my strongest assets. Start telling yourself that you have a wicked way with numbers, and in no time you will find them filling your head and helping you up the ladder.

3. I feel guilty because I've got so much

The beggars on the side of the road make you feel guilty, so you immediately hand over your sandwich, other than the bite in your mouth, or five bucks. The Guilt

Complex is one that leads to all sorts of self-deprivation in your business life. You don't push for the salary you're worth, because you're happy just to have a fabulous job. You're not worthy of the promotion, because someone worked harder than you. You shouldn't be on the incentive trip, because without your team you wouldn't have got there. You sacrifice yourself to support those you perceive to be less fortunate than you.

My incredible, enlightened Canadian friend Allan Meyer gave all – and I mean *all* – his money to help get the homeless off the streets of Los Angeles. He eventually had nothing left for himself. Two years later he went back to LA and found even more bums on the streets than before he'd started his crusade. His lesson? If you want to help the bums on the streets, stop feeding them. Share, by all means, but don't interfere in someone else's life lesson because, before you know it, you'll be learning *their* lesson.

Most of us do feel compassion for those less fortunate than ourselves, but you need to distinguish between compassion and guilt. Feel compassion by all means, but guilt is a damaging emotion. If you've got a lot, say a little prayer or meditation of gratitude every day to count your blessings. You are a very lucky person indeed. And the more you count your blessings, the luckier you will be.

4. I'm not good at sport

If you were an uncoordinated or chubby child, chances are you were left out of teams when it came to choose sides for a physical game. You eventually found that telling yourself you were no good at sport mollified your ego and you became – you guessed it – no good at sport. In the business context, this probably means you won't want to volunteer for challenging assignments or put your name forward for promotion for fear of being rejected or shown to be lacking. This hesitation, unfortunately, will bring your career to a grinding halt.

When was the last time you *really* tried to learn or play a sport? Maybe you're afraid of getting hurt, fair enough, but now's the time to go out and prove yourself wrong about your lack of ability. Find one sport or physical activity that you can be good at, and you'll suddenly find there are many others. Have you tried archery?

What about extreme ironing (get the riotous book *Extreme Ironing* by Phil Shaw)? Perhaps boules? A friend of ours, Geoff Earnshaw, has just received a Guinness World Record certificate for becoming the oldest person, at seventy, to abseil – and he chose the world's longest commercially available abseil to qualify. Geoff is built more like a brick sh*thouse than a sportsman and, to add insult to injury, he lost three or four of his fingers in a hijacking, which I'm convinced were sewn back onto the wrong joints.

5. I can't draw/paint/cook

My cooking skills extend to two-minute noodles. I suspect it's because I believe that I'm as creative as a blank wall. I have yet to overcome this bit of self-conditioning. 'I Can't Do This' or 'I'm No Good At That' is another notice you're sticking on your forehead that advertises your self-imposed limitations. If you walk around with a sign that says 'I Can't Strategise', then how the hell are you ever going to be considered for a management position?

My mate Ashley Marchment loves painting, but always told himself that he was 'rubbish'. At the age of forty-five, after studying how Vincent van Gogh was able to improve in only two years, Ashley decided that he, too, could become a 'great' painter, and he now exhibits his paintings in galleries and at exhibitions. Watch out for them – he signs his art Ashxxx. I think he's brilliant. His oils of the Antarctic are beautiful.

Here is an extract from Ashley's self-penned profile on the Artworx website:

Ashxxx's watercolour technique starts with pure contour drawing, where he com- pletes the full sketch without once taking his eyes off the subject (especially if she is a pretty girl) and without once looking at the drawing until it is finished. His earliest teacher was the late Wendy Amm, who asked him to please not tell anyone as she had a reputation to maintain. By mistake, his first large, exhibition painting was done using pure Mumm champagne instead of water. For his oils Ashxxx uses the new H2Oil paint, which is water-based oil. This prevents him from sip- ping turps instead of champagne when he paints. His art mentor and amateur psychoanalyst, Hanlie de Bondt's, favourite comment is, 'What I particularly like about your painting is one can see that you absolutely lose yourself in it. You get quite lost, don't you?' She also thinks he ought to be seeing a psycho-therapissed.

6. I can't lose weight

Don't you loathe those women who say, 'I can eat anything and I just don't put on weight'? Skinny cows. Having said that, there is one woman I know who can eat anything and not put on weight, and that is my lovely, willowy sister Carey Meredith.

In the main, I think most of the women who say that they can eat anything are lying. Equally, there is nothing really wrong with most who say they can't lose weight because of thyroid this, PCOS that. Who hasn't got a hormone problem of some sort? I watch my weight every single day of my life – and I'm hardly skinny. I'm devastated when I have a hormone blip, suffer from water retention or indulge and put on weight.

If you want to lose weight, it *is* a mission. But telling yourself that you can't lose weight usually means you won't even bother trying. Giving yourself an excuse makes it even worse. You will carry this same mindset into business with you. If you think something is going to be difficult or a real stretch, you won't want to try. A defeatist attitude will keep you tied to the bottom rungs of the ladder. Keep trying until you get it right.

Why is fat not good? One simple word – health. Find yourself a reputable professional to help you lose the weight and then watch what you put in your mouth for the rest of your life. As Brenda Bensted-Smith always reminds me, 'Nothing tastes as good as thin feels.'

7. I lack confidence

Deep down, we all have lapses of confidence. To the outside world we may appear self-assured and in control, but inside of us there is a flicker (or flame) of doubt. A flicker is normal. If your lack of confidence is such that it prevents you from leaving your house, accepting any social invitations or getting a job, you have a *big* problem and need professional help. If your crisis of confidence is less than this, you can fix it yourself. Take my friend Bobbie. She is beautiful (she looks like a blonde Cleopatra), slim, tall, warm, funny, enlightened (don't you hate her already?). Would a woman like this ever doubt herself? It may surprise you to hear that even a woman as deliciously savvy and well adjusted as Bobbie lacks confidence from time to time.

In the business world, these flickers of self-doubt are fine, but be aware if they are holding you back. Only you will know. A lack of confidence will make you reluctant to push your boundaries. It will make you resistant to change, make you want to stay in your comfort zone. This does not help you to grow, to self-actualise. Shake off those doubts and just do it, as the Nike adverts say.

There are plenty of women who, for reasons unimaginable, lack self-assurance. The best quick fix for this is the following: Every single time you catch yourself saying *anything* negative about yourself – especially *to* yourself – consciously replace what you are saying with something positive. You may struggle to do this in the beginning, partly because you won't be able to think of positive things quickly enough, and partly because of modesty, but persevere. You'll soon get into the habit and your self-confidence will start turning the corner. Do not give in to that part of your conscious that tells you you're being vain – tell it to get back in its hole.

8. I was a bad student, so I won't go far in life

There are two sides to this belief. The first is conditioning. When my sister Carey was young and impressionable, she was told that she would be a 'C-stream' student. Guess what? She was a 'C-stream' student. But Carey is smart. If she had been told that she would be an 'A-streamer', I firmly believe she would have been in the 'A' class. She has done incredibly well in the business world, achieving way beyond what she was programmed to expect of herself. She has overcome her conditioning.

The second belief is that if you did badly as a student, you won't excel in the work environment. This is often self-conditioning – we convince ourselves we won't do well. The scary part is that these paradigms are usually formed when we are teenagers and we end up with a teenager having made the decision on how we will perform as an adult. There are so many reasons why people don't excel at school, so few of which have anything to do with ability. The list of the wealthiest people in the world changes from month to month (and from source to source), but did you know that on a recent list, only three of the world's richest had completed a tertiary education?

What conditioning are you living? Your own? A teacher's or a parent's, or maybe a husband's? Take stock of what nonsense has been put in your head and tell yourself: 'If Bill Gates can get ahead after being branded a dropout and a failure, I can do it too!'

9. I can't sell

Without the ability to sell, you are not able to function properly in life. If you can't sell, you won't get a job or a life-partner or friends, or that promotion or the big deal that you want. You can't just sit there and hope that someone will notice you and choose you to be his bride or recruit you for a fabulous job. You have to sell yourself. You have to be able to convince someone else – whether through your verbal, physical, sexual or intellectual skills – that you are who they want.

Has the light come on yet that selling is part of what we do every day of our lives? Don't be scared of selling in the world of work. You don't necessarily have to take a job as a salesperson; you just need to appreciate that part of what everyone does involves selling in some form or another: Convincing the board to implement your new ideas; persuading someone to take a job; winning over an adversary. These are all forms of selling.

Some people practise more and are thus better at selling – but it takes practice to make perfect. Kissing the Blarney Stone does not help (I have tried). Neither does being born with the 'gift of the gab' – these people tend to talk too much and listen too little, and thus are not as successful at selling as you may imagine. Attend a sales course, even if you're a secretary (start by selling your boss on the idea as your first test), to notch up the level of your game. Being able to convince people to give you what you want means that you rely less on the more difficult skills of negotiating, power-adjusting, conflict management, and so on.

10. I'm a hopeless negotiator

With this mindset, you can't negotiate! Sure, negotiation is difficult. It's a skill most people seem to have lost along the way. Lost? We are all – each and every one of us – born brilliant negotiators. Don't for a moment believe the rubbish that says negotiators are taught, not born. Cast your mind back to when you were a child and you wanted a treat – maybe to be taken to the park or to have a chocolate before dinner. How did you get what you wanted? You first tried the kid versions of selling, which would have been throwing a tantrum if you were two years old, or begging if you were four: 'Pleeeease can I have a chocolate?' Or manipulation if you were five: 'I love you, Mommy. Please may I have a chocolate? I'll share it with you.' Aha! The first signs of negotiation emerge.

Children peak as negotiators from the age of six to about eight years old. If you have children of this age, you will know exactly what I am talking about. How do they do it? Firstly, they are born with negotiation skills. Secondly, kids do not apply associative logic to negotiations. Here's an example. Mom: 'Johnny, go to bed.' Johnny: 'If you take me to the park on Saturday, I'll go to bed in five minutes.' How did he manage to link the park to bedtime? Who taught Johnny how to trade? We all have an innate ability to negotiate – we just need to relearn our lost skills. Imagine how far being a great negotiator can take you up the ladder? And you'll be earning the best possible salary along the way.

Here's a delightful little story from a course my organisation conducts on deal-making, in which we teach people to synthesise selling and negotiating. We encourage the course delegates to practise what they learn on the course at home each night. On the third day of the course, one of the participants walked into the lecture room with a huge grin. He had outsmarted his three-year-old. His son, who was already in bed, was saying that he was not going to go to sleep. Dad replied: 'If you close your eyes, you don't have to go to sleep.' A few minutes later, the three-year-old was fast asleep.

11. I've got a bad memory

I have an excellent memory for details relating to music and movies. Ask me who sang or wrote what song in nineteen-*voetsek*, and I can tell you. Ask me who played what role in a movie I haven't even seen and I can tell you. But ask me who directed the movie, and I'm rubbish. Ask me what the turnover is of my company, or the price of our products, and I have only a vague idea. Why is my memory good in some areas and bad in others? I used to think it was about one's level of interest in a subject, but that theory's been disproved. I'm passionate about my business and about films, so bang goes that theory. I believe it's because I've told myself that I am good at remembering certain things and haven't told myself I'm good at the others.

How many times a day do you tell someone, including yourself, that you have a bad memory? Our memory supposedly fades with time. I think a brain is like a filing cabinet made up of billions upon billions of little drawers. In each drawer is a memory or piece of information. The information we access regularly keeps those little drawers sliding smoothly. Accessing memories we haven't recalled for some time requires us to jiggle the drawers a bit before we can get to the memory. Then there is information in drawers we think are stuck shut forever.

When I was studying psychology, I read the case of a German man who had moved to the USA as a young boy. On arriving in America, he could speak no English. Sixty years later he could remember no German, but spoke fluent English. Age seventy or so, he had a brain tumour removed and woke from the anaesthetic speaking fluent German. He could recall no English. This, to my mind, proves my drawer theory and challenges the theory that we lose our memory as we get older. We lose only our ability to open the drawers. Keep those drawers well oiled with crosswords and Sudoku, and by telling yourself that it's all in there somewhere.

12. I'll lose my friends if I'm successful

As you rise up the ladder, you may well lose friends along the way. There will be those who feel threatened by your success, and there'll be friends who are so proud of you they could burst. Do you really need the friends who are jealous and want to hold you back? The bitches who are miserable when your star is in its ascendancy and gleeful when you are having a hard time? Rise to the top and leave them behind. True friends want their friends to be happy and successful.

A couple of things to watch for. Firstly, if *you* are the jealous friend who resents the success being achieved by your friends, you need to revisit your 'bad' list and take a serious look at your behaviour. Envy and bitterness will eat away at you and bring the worst of your being to the fore. Secondly, as you rise in the ranks, remember to retain your essence and a modicum of modesty. Nobody likes a big shot. Not even Mr Big.

The reason these twelve lies are on the list of ways for a Work Diva to screw up her career is because getting ahead in the workplace is hard enough without you being your own worst enemy. Stop the lies and stop being unkind to yourself, and you will see a new you start to emerge – a Work Diva of worth.

4: IT'S BECAUSE I'M NOT A MAN

'A male gynaecologist is like an auto mechanic who has never owned a car.'   – *Carrie Snow (American stand-up comedienne; 1953–?)*

We have discussed this subject before, so why does it reappear on the Big Five list of how to mess up your career? Because it's really important and needs more attention. 'Then why is it not on the list of lies people tell themselves?' you may ask. The lies are just that – lies. This one happens to be true to a large extent. Much has been done to overcome the gender divide in business, but inequality still exists. If, given this inequality, you allow yourself to subscribe to the school of 'It's because I'm not a man', then you *will* screw up your career.

Although you may be told that inequality is a thing of the past, it's still very much a reality. Take this classic example: I joined a company in the late 1990s as executive director of strategy. I was the only woman on a board of eight people, but at the same level as my co-directors. First board meeting: The tea lady brings in a tray, puts it down on the sideboard and leaves the room. Seven men look at me. I had a couple of choices:

– I could get up, help myself to tea and sit down again, offering no one else tea, or

- I could fit the stereotype and get up and pour for everyone, or
- I could look back at them and say, 'Well, who's going to pour?'

I got up and offered everyone tea. I can hear you calling me a sell-out!

Let me explain why I poured the tea. I expect men to stand aside and let me pass first through a door. I expect them to open my car door and hold the elevator for me. I like it if they stand up when I enter a room. I have my own expectations of men, just as they have their expectations of me. It's the natural order, to my mind – and just basic good manners. It really irritates me when some healthy young guy leaps onto a bus or train and beats the woman, older or not, to a seat. I think it's just plain boorish behaviour. I'm saddened when I think that with equality comes the loss of decent manners and of respecting the differences between men and women.

While men can be accused of having their own rules of conduct for the office, women are just as guilty in the games they play and behaviours they display. Here, according to author Riley Klein, are the 'Biggest Mistakes Women Make At Work' (from Part 1 of a series titled *A Career Woman's Guide to Shattering the Glass Ceiling*, extracted from www.howtodothings.com):

1. Trapping yourself in a non-business role

Think about it. Do you scold people for leaving a big mess in the break room, then clean up behind them (mother role)? Do you plan potlucks at the office, then expect the guys to contribute equally by bringing in a dish (wife role)? Are you always asking for help or advice from men, unable to make a decision on your own (daughter role)? Is there a particular guy you like to tease and to goof off with (flirt role)? Do you dress suggestively, wearing low-cut blouses with cleavage, tight pants, or short skirts (sex siren role)? If you've trapped yourself into any of these traditional female roles, it's no wonder the guys can't take you seriously!

2. Bringing inappropriate girl behaviour to the office

Do you socialise at work, gossiping about other people? Do you spend work time discussing your last vacation, your kids' accomplishments, or your husband's faults? Do you have to 'catch up' with all the other gals about office politics? Have you ever been caught painting your nails, doing your hair, or applying make-up in your office? Were you involved in a catty feud with another lady at the office? Are you critical of others, complaining and whining? Do others think you're too bossy or nit-picky? If any of these describe you, wake up, Sister! How do you expect to earn the respect of your progressive colleagues when the office is merely your extended social and domestic circle?

3. Trying to be 'one of the boys'

Do you join the guys for drinks after work, hoping to be seen as one of them? Do you laugh at their crude jokes to try to fit in? Do you follow the guys around, trying to imitate everything they do, hoping someone will recognise your accomplishments? If so, you're sure to annoy them, irritate your boss, and evoke the jealousy of the other women in the office. You certainly won't be accepted as one of 'them,' but you may get known as a 'kiss-up'! Here's a tip: Don't try to 'fit in' by copying men. You'll never be one of them. In fact, you don't want to. And the good news is that (whew!) you don't have to! You can be successful on your own terms.

4. Thinking too small

Men in leadership positions are 'big picture' oriented, and can become frustrated when you constantly dwell on the details. But if you get a reputation for being the 'dream killer,' you'll never be part of the 'inside' team of decision makers.

5. Failing to understand and respect men's viewpoint

Men think differently than women. Period. Don't try to persuade them to think like you do. Appreciate and respect their perspective – you don't have to understand 'why.' Be cautious about telling 'men' jokes and belittling the guys at the office. They think differently, they communicate differently, they view 'teamwork' differently, they express themselves differently, they relate differently, and they arrive at different solutions. They're not better or worse. Just different. And that's okay.

If someone tells you the glass ceiling does not exist, tell them that the only person they're fooling is themself. It *is* there, but we divas owe it to ourselves, and to all the other women out there, to smash it to bits with our handbags. What's the best way to do this? To succeed as women in business, we need to work harder and smarter than the men. We need to be better read, better prepared, better everything. I know it's not fair – life is not fair (see chapter on 'victim mentality'!). Get smashing, girl.

5: NETWORKING IS OVERRATED

'A personal network is like a safety net, hanging beneath the high
perch of the tightrope walker.' – *Cynthia Chin-Lee*
(American author and speaker)

The subject of networking has already been mentioned, but it deserves much more than merely a mention. Networking is an art. Networking is a science. Networking will give you the push you need to climb the corporate ladder faster than those around you. 'It's not what you know, it's who you know' is an oft-quoted saying. Nowadays it should be: 'It's what you know *and* who you know.'

As women, we have a natural ability to communicate and nurture relationships. This ability is the very foundation of social networking and thus a great asset in the business world. Why, then, do so many people shy away from networking? Why do people justify their reluctance to network on the grounds of networking not being that important? Not important? It's critical. But, that said, it is the quality of your network that counts, not just having any old network.

Earlier I quoted Robert Appelbaum, one of South Africa's top attorneys, as saying, 'Intelligent social networking is the key to success.' Every book, publication and paper says the same thing: quality networking is essential. Have a look on the internet and you will be met by a barrage of articles on the importance of networking. Point made?

Why is networking so vital? In her book *It's Who You Know*, Cynthia Chin-Lee quotes Adele Scheele, author of *Skills for Success*, as saying:

There are so many different reasons for creating and maintaining connections to others and their organisations. Connecting gives us perspective about how we work, provides us with different approaches to problems and sharpens our ideas of what is important, relevant, or new. Contacts also release us from a feeling of dependence, allowing us to be bolder in our thinking because we are no longer afraid that ours is the only job in the entire system. All told, connecting with others is enriching and life-giving, and assures us of endless possibility and opportunity.

Cynthia Chin-Lee herself goes on to say:

A good example of effective networking is the 'old-boy network'. Originally the members of the old-boy network were the sons of blue-blood or aristocratic families in the United States. They attended exclusive preparatory schools in New England and then the Ivy League colleges. After graduation these fellows took care of one another; they referred their former classmates to top jobs and best opportunities available in the country.

Networking works as a system for connecting people, for their benefit and your own. Think of it like a circus, with you as the ringmaster. You choose who belongs to your circus based on what they bring to the show. You pair your performers with other acts to bring out the best in each other. You select specific skills for certain acts, and other skills for different parts of the show. When you need to recruit new staff, you get the members of your team to give you names of other brilliant performers they know.

If you decide to leave your circus, you know who owns which circuses, so you can choose who to approach for interviews. If the circus-owners know about you, they approach you, or ask for your input in their hiring decisions. The ultimate test of being a brilliant networker is that you never get into the job-hunt market. You move from circus to circus with the world as your merry-go-round.

That's all good and well, but how does one actually go about networking? Let's start from ground zero – where to begin? Having 'Driver' as my behavioural style did not always serve me well in the early days of my career. I hated going to business-related social functions and had no idea how to conduct polite conversation with a total stranger. I was ordered to a Hewlett-Packard cocktail party by Bob Strain, one of my early mentors, and told to 'learn to network'. Initiation by fire.

At the function, I homed in on a non-threatening-looking individual standing alone, marched up to him and demanded to know his name, company, position – sort of army style. The poor man, completely alarmed, complied. I did calm down, with the help of a few glasses of red wine, and was soon chatting away about his job, his family and his dogs. 'This is not so difficult!' I thought. My first attempt had not been a complete disaster, but, as you can see, hardly a resounding success. I continued to practise my 'conversations with strangers', and eventually found that I *liked* talking to people and finding out about their lives. Today, I *love* talking to people and delving into their passions, their ambitions, their hopes and dreams – anything that gets them animated and fired up.

Once you've taken that first step, it will get easier. If you are naturally interested in other people, you already have an advantage. When starting out on your 'net-working' career, you may want to play it safe and ask questions about the other person's job, family, dogs, holidays and so on. As you become more adept, try to find out what motivates the person to get up in the morning. What they would do differently with their lives if they were suddenly twenty-one again. What pizza topping they would be if they were a pizza.

You will know that you've got the hang of it when you can have a conversation with someone and do *not* use the question 'So what do you do?' as your opening gambit. What they 'do' will come out in the course of the conversation, but test yourself – see if you can have a decent chat without using this question. To keep my networking conversational skills sharp, I now actively avoid talking about what people do or what I do and focus instead on their personal drivers. As I've said before, it's amazing what people will tell you if you just ask.

When you start developing your network, you may not be able to discern the difference between a quality business contact and simply a contact. That's fine – don't give up. As your network grows, you will learn to distinguish between who is nice to know and who you need to know to help you build your own circus. You will find that you're ringmaster to all sorts of mini-circuses – people to supply your company, people who will buy from you, people to partner with or distribute your products, where to source the most outrageous of items, and so on.

So is networking overrated? Not a chance.

Chapter 12

RUNG 9:
BEFORE YOU REACH FOR THE TOP RUNG

IS THIS REALLY WHAT YOU WANT?

> 'Getting to the top is optional, but getting down is mandatory. A lot
> of people get focused on the summit and forget that.'
>
> *— Ed Viesturs (one of the world's premier*
> *high-altitude mountaineers; 1959–?)*

Before you reach for that top rung, you need to take a long, hard look at what will
be expected of you if you go for the summit, so to speak. Expectations people have
of you when you reach the top are very different from what is required of you while
you are climbing the ladder. It's tough at the top. It's not all glamorous international travel, board meetings where you can strut your stuff, having a great office
and being able to afford a swanky car. You have to make heart-breaking decisions,
your values will be continuously tested and you need to survive corporate politics
that make general office politics look like a day at the beach.

At the top, you sell your life to your company. Work–life balance? Great in
theory, but it's not available to the top dogs. Except Richard Branson. Maybe. This
chapter is designed to make you think about whether being at the top is really

what you want. Be prepared – your paradigms and preconceived ideas are going to be seriously challenged.

When I talked about my own career path earlier in the book, I said that a driving passion for business is what helped me climb to the top of my tree. If you don't have a passion for the cut and thrust of the business world burning inside – and we're not talking about big fat salaries and fancy job titles here – then sorry, sweetheart, but that last rung is probably not going to happen for you.

Important question: What *is* driving you to climb the ladder? You need to recognise what is motivating you and then decide if the business world is going to give you what you want. Will it satisfy the fire inside of you? If a nice big salary cheque is what inspires you, then chase the money. You can make much – and I mean *much* – more money as a professional salesperson. The top salespeople I know earn three or four times the salaries of their managing directors, sometimes more. Brokers and traders also make an absolute killing, if they are any good. Is your passion to change the world? Maybe a career in politics or charities like the Red Cross or UNICEF would be a better choice. If fame and glory keep you feverish with excitement, consider the performing arts or being a spin doctor (or a politician) of some sort.

If in response to the 'What is driving you?' question you answered 'Success', you need to define exactly what success means to you. You can achieve success as a cyclist. Did you say job satisfaction? Again, define the specifics – you can do any job and get satisfaction – you don't have to be at the top of the ladder. Working for Greenpeace and sinking the fishing trawlers that damage the world's dolphin population would give me immense satisfaction! Recognition? Influence? Define what these mean to you and then check if the business world is really where you should be. Try to whittle down your answer to one or two tangible specifics to the question of what is driving you, then check and double-check that the corporate world is really where you want to make your mark.

Still determined to forge ahead in the business world? Good for you. Here come the real tests.

SELLING YOUR LIFE, NOT YOUR SOUL

> 'The secret of success is making your vocation your vacation.'
> — *Samuel Langhorne Clemens, aka Mark Twain*
> *(American author; 1835–1910)*

You may have thought I was being flippant when I said you have to 'sell your life to your company'. I wish I was, but I'm not. The whole point of this book is how to get to the top of the ladder *without* selling your soul. But what about selling your life? That's another story.

When you reach the top of the tree – and I do mean the top (middle management means just that – the middle) – your job will demand a huge amount from you. If you have the attitude, 'When I reach the top, I'm going to kick off my Manolos and enjoy the fruits of my hard work,' you won't have long to enjoy the fruits, because before you know it, you'll be kicked off your branch. As I've said, the real work starts when you get to the top. You may know one or two people who are at the top and taking life easy. Keep an eye on them and your climbing shoes at the ready. They won't be there for long.

If you are starting to get nervous about the consequences of reaching the very top, let me reassure you on an important point. If, for you, 'the top' is middle management – being a manager rather than an executive – there is no shame in that. If you are prepared to sell yourself only *to a point*, then middle management is the perfect goal. Don't let anyone tell you otherwise. Being head of public relations or purchasing or IT is great. You may not want to become the CIO if your passion is for the technology, rather than the strategic issues – and you still want a life.

Let's take a look at the habits of executives in large organisations. They are the last to leave the office. The demands of their jobs are such that they can't work the proverbial 'nine to five'. They may leave the office at six o'clock in the evening so that they can kiss little Johnny goodnight, but after Johnny is in bed, they fire up their laptops and work. On the weekends they entertain, but there are invariably some boring work associates banging on at the dinner table. Remember I told you about Patrick the Redhead? He is the country manager of a large global IT company (no, not the same one that employs Ms Porn Star). Five out of seven nights *every* week, Patrick entertains business associates. Sometimes with spouses, sometimes without. Patrick has an amazing wife, whom he loves dearly. Trust me, he would rather be at home with her than with some businessman who won't hesitate to cast Patrick aside if the company falls on hard times. Patrick has a life-threatening disease and needs to watch his diet, but he entertains to keep the organisation at the top of its market. His health takes a back seat.

Another very dear friend of mine, who shall remain nameless because he'll kill me if I even hint at who he is, had a wife, two small children and a business to build. His wife took care of the kids; he grew the business. Seven years later he was managing director of one of the most successful business units of a huge global corporation. He'd made a lot of money, but his relationship with his wife was over and his kids had no real bond with him. He took a sabbatical to spend time nurturing the relationship with his children, but teenagers don't really want their father hanging around. He managed to build a great bond with his kids, but will only go back to work when they have their own lives.

I can recite story after story about the cost of being at the top of the ladder. Most are sad and most are about men, but that's because most C-level executives are men. Why do men hold these positions? Mostly because business is male-dominated, but also because women aren't always willing to pay the price the top job demands. Can you see why I suggested early on in this book that women should choose between kids and career?

When it comes to work–life balance, executives don't even get a look-in. A lot of companies, particularly large global ones, will have a core value that goes something like this: 'Work–life balance is essential for a fully functioning team. It is a value we passionately strive to respect and maintain,' or some other bull. Why do I say it's bull? Because I can't name *one* – no, not even one – organisation that honours this maxim. They all seem to have lovely motivational posters stuck up on the walls espousing this value, but when the going gets tough, these companies want their pound of flesh and more.

I have no problem with companies demanding their pounds of flesh – most people can choose where to work in the corporate world – but why the hypocrisy? Because it drives up share prices. Companies with good corporate values impress the investor market. Welcome to the real corporate world, Work Diva.

Why, then, you may be wondering, does Mr Big fight so hard to stay at the top? Why doesn't he just *get a life*? If this is where your head is at, go back to my question in the previous section where I asked, 'What is driving you?' If, however, despite what I have told you, you are still passionate about the business world and are resolute about climbing to the top, then read on. You may have to sell yourself to your job, but you don't have to lose your soul.

WILL YOU FIND A BOWL OF CHERRIES?

> 'Whenever you see a successful business, someone once made a courageous decision.'
> — *Dr Peter F Drucker*
> *(American management theorist and author; 1909–2005)*

There is an old cartoon that shows a man, having just climbed to the summit of a mountain, saying to the cross-legged guru sitting at the top, 'That's it? Life's a bowl of cherries?' You've obviously figured out by now that life at the top of the ladder is anything but a bowl of cherries. Still determined to get to the top? Good for you.

Here is a list of the nine key attributes you will need to master when you are at the top of the ladder. This is not a list from which you get to pick and choose what you will or won't do – this is a list of qualities you *must* demonstrate.

1. Lose the right to 'rights'

As an executive, you have to let go of your 'rights' – your right to lunch times, to tea breaks, to be paid for overtime, to set working hours, to regular vacations. People who have a 'rights' mentality, rather than a 'responsibilities' mindset, don't do well in the boardroom. They are seen as egocentric and lacking in emotional intelligence. At the top, you have responsibilities to your organisation and to all the stakeholders. It is not about 'me, me, me'.

2. Being self-reliant

It is lonely at the top. Not only must executives of large organisations give up their 'rights', but they need to be self-reliant. This means that they are required to depend on their own capabilities and judgements. Alison Gomme, a leading British prison governor, is quoted as saying, 'Being the boss anywhere is lonely. Being a female boss in a world of mostly men is especially so.' Prepare for the loneliness – especially if you are going to be CEO of your own organisation. There is no lonelier place in the corporate world.

No matter how good you are at your job or how charming a person you may be, there will be people who don't like you or won't support you, simply because you are at the top. People can be very jealous of success. If being Ms Popularity is important to you, get used to the idea now that no matter what you do or don't do, there will be people who simply dislike you for no good reason at all.

3. A strategic outlook

Executives usually earn a lot more money than the people below them. Why? Because they are paid for their ability to think strategically and deliver results based on these strategies. If you think the pay disparity is unfair, consider it this way: an executive can sweep a floor, but can a floor sweeper run an organisation? At the top of the ladder you get paid for your abilities to strategise, lead and build. Maybe, if the floor sweeper had been given all the opportunities for education and development, she, too, would be able to run the organisation. The point is that she doesn't, so she can't expect to earn the same salary or be given the same position. It raises its head again – the importance of development. Are you developing your strategic thinking skills?

A strategic outlook means that you focus on the big picture (usually external issues), not the day-to-day operational (usually internal) issues. Managers are operational, whereas executives are strategic. As my husband Simon describes it, executives work *on* the business rather than *in* the business. Executives make sure things get done, but they don't do those things themselves. This brings us to three new points: managing vs leading, delegation and people selection.

4. Managers vs leaders

Stephen R Covey, author of *The 7 Habits of Highly Effective People*, says that 'management is efficiency in climbing the ladder of success; leadership determines whether the ladder is leaning against the right wall'. A leader is like the conductor of an orchestra, whereas the managers are the principals responsible for running each instrumental section. When people buy classical music, they want to know the name of the conductor rather than the orchestra, because different conductors can draw very different performances from the same orchestra. Just like a change in the big boss can completely change the culture of an organisation.

I found the following useful chart on www.changingminds.org. The table summarises the differences between being a leader and being a manager. They make the point that 'many people lead and manage at the same time, and so may display a combination of behaviours'.

SUBJECT	LEADER	MANAGER
Essence	Change	Stability
Focus	Leading people	Managing work
Have	Followers	Subordinates
Horizon	Long term	Short term
Seeks	Vision	Objectives
Approach	Sets direction	Plans detail
Decision	Facilitates	Makes
Power	Personal charisma	Formal authority
Appeal to	Heart	Head

SUBJECT	LEADER	MANAGER
Energy	Passion	Control
Dynamic	Proactive	Reactive
Persuasion	Sell	Tell
Style	Transformational	Transactional
Exchange	Excitement for work	Money for work
Likes	Striving	Action
Wants	Achievement	Results
Risk	Takes	Minimises
Rules	Breaks	Makes
Conflict	Uses	Avoids
Direction	New roads	Existing roads
Truth	Seeks	Establishes
Concern	What is right	Being right
Credit	Gives	Takes
Blame	Takes	Blames

5. Delegation

Whether you are a manager or a leader, you must be able to delegate. Women are not the greatest delegators. We're so used to multitasking and doing things for our friends and families, and particularly our children, that we don't always think about delegating. In addition, women ask themselves questions such as, 'Why should I get someone else to do it when I am perfectly capable of doing it myself?' or 'I feel bad loading another person with all this work,' or how about, 'What if they don't do it as well as I can?' These questions may stem from guilt and, to a small extent, from not being able to say no, but not wanting to delegate is typically associated with not wanting to lose control.

Delegating to others empowers them, freeing you up to focus on strategic issues. At the top you *have* to be able to delegate – and keep the people to whom you are delegating motivated to perform the tasks or projects to the best of their ability. It is, by the way, much easier to delegate down than sideways or up. Delegating to colleagues or bosses is thorny and requires a lot of planning before you approach them.

6. Hiring and firing

The most successful executives surround themselves with the best people they can find. It is essential for executives to recruit people who complement their own styles. If an executive is, for argument's sake, not a brilliant orator, he or she will include in their top team a person who is a gifted speaker.

I was recently having a conversation along these lines with an executive at one of the planet's biggest IT companies. Let's call him Garth. Garth has assembled a really talented team of people. When I asked Garth on what basis he recruited people for his team, he replied that he likes to hire individuals who are smarter than him. Now Garth is no slouch in the intelligence stakes, so I think this must be extremely difficult, but that's what a good executive will do. They are not threatened by the people around them being better than they are. Having the best possible team allows them to consistently deliver great results. Insecure executives tend to surround themselves with weaker people – often yes-men (who agree with everything they say and don't challenge them), or those with skills that won't threaten their position. Insecure executives usually fail to present good results and will thus ultimately lose their positions.

On the subject of losing jobs, executives must be able to make tough firing decisions. If someone is not bringing in the expected results, despite performance-management efforts, the big boss will need to dismiss that person – regardless of whether he or she has an invalid mother, an unemployed partner and four children to support. Will you be able to do this? Will you be able to remove those from your organisation who damage the company's ability to perform? What if it's a close friend or a relative? You don't have a choice – you *have* to take the firing decision.

7. Decisions, decisions

At the top of the ladder, you are the decisions you make. And, as you can see, you will have to make some pretty unpleasant ones. These will test the essence of your value system. What happens when you have to support a decision with which you disagree – such as executing a strategy decided upon by your board that you don't personally back? How about making a decision that may have short-term benefits, but will bring significant negative ramifications further down the line?

You are on your own at the top, so, while you might ask people for their opinion, it is leadership they will want from you, not dithering or uncertainty. There is a school of thought that says it's better to make a wrong decision than to make no decision at all. What do you think? An essential requirement of leaders is that they are able to make decisions, even at the risk of these being wrong. By the by, making no decision is still a decision of sorts.

According to www.mindtools.com:

If you want to lead effectively, you need to be able to make good decisions. If you can learn to do this in a timely and well-considered way, then you can lead your team to spectacular and well-deserved success. However, if you dither or make poor decisions, your team risks failure and your time as a leader will probably be brutally short.

8. Dealing with conflict

No balanced person enjoys conflict. If you are completely conflict-averse, the top is definitely not for you. You will face conflict every day, and you need to handle it with good judgement and maturity. If you avoid the conflict, hoping it will eventually go away, it more often than not simply festers and leads to a massive problem. You have to act quickly and decisively with conflict.

Conflict resolution is emotionally draining. Many years ago, Patrick the Redhead called me in to resolve a problem in his company. He had two super-bright software developers working for him. They had been great friends until the woman, Gail, discovered that her colleague, Sam, had been a member of the National Front in England (a right-wing group associated with Nazism) in his youth. Gail had lost her grandparents in the Holocaust.

On finding this out about Sam's background, although he now actively denounced the National Front, Gail refused to work with him. I had to resolve this conflict. The situation was so bad that only one of them could stay in the company. What would you have done? Whom would you have dismissed? You will be dealing with conflicts far worse than this when you get into the boardroom.

9. The unglamorous side of the top

In my last corporate board position I got to travel the globe, attend glamorous parties and events, meet exciting people, eat in the best restaurants in the world, drink cocktails in exotic locations. Of course it was fabulous fun, but there was a downside. International travel involves sitting in soulless airports for hours on end and catching bugs on the aircraft (I'm talking sick bugs, not the huge, smelly, voluble passengers you end up sitting next to. It's never a cute guy – I've concluded that they have their own secret airline). Next comes the lost luggage (I once, stupidly, packed all my trousers and skirts in one bag and my tops and jackets in another – and, you guessed it, only one bag got to London with me), and then the rude airline staff, delayed flights, packing, unpacking, packing, unpacking.

You're still saying to yourself that you can deal with that? Wait, there's more. At cocktail parties dirty old men proposition you and pinch your bum. You get fat and sick from what you eat, you drink more than you should and spend most of your time with people *not* of your choice. Still fun? How about the very hard work that goes with the travel, in countries where you don't understand the culture or the corporate games? Trust me, when your company sends you overseas, they want to make the most of their investment in air fares and hotels, so you have breakfast meetings, lunch meetings, dinner meetings and meetings in between. You fall into bed and then start the merry cycle again the next day. You arrive home shattered.

And then there are the board meetings. I am going to start a campaign to rename them 'bored meetings'. Boy, do some of the geezers like the sound of their own voices or what? It's not all cut and thrust – a big chunk of it is posturing, pontificating and just plain bulldusting. You feel, sometimes, that you are bleeding from your eyeballs in your efforts to stay awake.

What tipped me over the edge – bearing in mind that I was eventually travelling for six months of every year for nearly nine years – was the personal price I had to pay. I ended up with an ulcer, a fat ass and a dog that had become deeply depressed. And I missed my home and my man so much that I thought my heart would break.

Being at the top is stimulating, demanding, exhausting – and it can be fun, but with that fun comes a huge price tag. Are you ready to pay the price? If you are unsure, step back and think long and hard about grabbing that last rung.

Chapter 13

THE TOP RUNG:
HOW NOT TO SELL YOUR SOUL

LIFTING YOUR SPIRITS

'If life is a bowl of cherries, then what am I doing in the pits?'

– Erma Bombeck
(American humorist and columnist; 1927–1996)

Climbing the ladder is difficult and there will be times when it's going to get you down. You need to find ways and means of picking yourself up and dusting yourself off. But how, when you're in the doldrums, can you find the means to restore your spirit? It's not that easy to do, is it? You need to create your own little pick-me-up recipes, but here are a few ideas that I find helpful, fun and, most of all, uplifting.

1. Music, movies and books

These are three of my all-time favourite therapies to cure the blues. They have proven to be such valuable outlets for me that the next section of the book is dedicated to them. You can find music, movies and books for all your blue moods, from slightly 'miz' to downright manic. Learn to recognise which ones help you release your pent-up emotions, and you'll find an unexpected form of liberation.

2. Cocktails and champagne (or coffee, if you prefer)

There is something fabulously decadent about a colourful cocktail with an umbrella. It's a truly cheerful sight, as is a beautiful glass (have you seen the Versace-designed Rosenthal crystal champagne flutes?) filled with sparkling French bubbles. I'm as happy sipping a cocktail or a glass of champagne in my own backyard watching the dogs play as I am sitting at a café in Camps Bay overlooking the sea. Whether on your own or with a friend or loved one, taking a few minutes out to enjoy a simple pleasure is good for the soul. If you're not into alcohol, lots of women find the same contentment in a cup of coffee while watching their kids. Savour the moment.

3. Relish a meal

Whether you've cooked it yourself or not (definitely *not* in my case), there is great joy in sharing a meal with someone special, or savouring the flavours and aromas of a delicious dish on your own. Do you have a favourite restaurant – a place that holds fond memories and whose food you love? If not, try to find one. It can become a sanctuary of sorts, if you choose the right space. You don't have to bust the diet or the budget. The same amount of happiness can be found in a mouthful of chocolate cake as in eating the whole thing. Have you ever eaten proper baked cheesecake in New York? If you have, you'll know exactly what I'm talking about. If not, put it on your list of things to do in your life. Last time I was in New York, I skipped breakfast every day in favour of this particular heaven.

4. Good friends

After having an operation last year, I was feeling very sorry for myself. My friends Brenda Bensted-Smith, Nicola Jackson and Karen Evans came to the house one evening, armed with champagne and sympathy (no food, mind you). The four of us drank four bottles of champagne and laughed until we hurt. My surgeon was not a happy man when I arrived the next morning for a check-up. 'You've been drinking,' he said accusingly. How did he know? My wound was too swollen for the fancy plastic bandage thing he had used – but it sure was worth it!

5. Bad friends

This is going to be hard to do.

- Write down the names of all – yes *all* – your friends.
- Next, write down the two or three qualities that are really important to you in a friendship, such as:
  - your friends must love you unconditionally, or
  - they must always be there for you, or
  - they must be generous of spirit, or
  - you must be able to trust them completely, or
  - whatever it is that is important to *you* in a friendship.
- Then, rank each of your friends against these qualities on a scale of one to ten, where one out of ten is a lousy match, five is okay and ten is a perfect score.
- Highlight the people who have an *average* score of seven or more. These are the people in whom you should invest your time and energy. If they are not special friends, they should be, so make plans to bring them closer into your life.
- Anyone who scores an average of four or less needs to move off your friendship list. You can take the Driver approach and terminate the friendships post-haste, or you can take the Amiable road and slowly and kindly work them out. The choice is yours, but go they must.
- For those who score five or six, start terminating the close friendships and moving them to 'acquaintances' status.

'But these are my friends!' I hear you cry. Are they really? Would they do everything in their power to ensure your happiness? No? Then sorry, they are not true friends. The sooner you can rid yourself of the energy vampires, takers, deceivers, etc., the sooner your life will brighten.

6. Talk about it

Talk to someone – someone who loves you and will not judge you. Someone who will be completely and unconditionally on your side. If you're even vaguely suicidal, that someone may need to be a professional, but talking is sharing and sharing really does lighten the load. Nicola Jackson, undoubtedly the most gorgeous legal professional in the country, suggests that you surround yourself with positive people whom you love and trust. 'Talk to them, get advice and let them tell you how damn fabulous you really are!' Nicola says. She believes that this will put things in perspective and pull you out of your state of misery and self-pity. I think she's on the money!

7. Time on your own

There are going to be times when you want your friends around you, and there are going to be times when you need to be on your own. If you find that you *always* call on your friends when you are down, it will be good for your soul to try to work through a few issues by yourself. We all need quiet time to reflect and contemplate life (you can also call this meditation, or prayer, if you prefer). Perhaps, just perhaps, being down in the dumps is the soul's way of slowing us down and forcing us into a little self-reflection. If you don't get this time alone because you need your friends to pull you out of your misery, you're missing out on a wonderful opportunity for quality 'me' time. There is tremendous power in this type of solitude – unleash the power and you will find your mood starts to shift.

8. Pamper yourself

With all the day and health spas around, it is really easy – and not too expensive – to take yourself off for a treatment or two. If your budget (and time) allows, go for the entire day and have the whole works – jacuzzi, sauna, facial, manicure, pedicure, massage, blow-dry. But, go on your own. Use the time to reflect or to think about absolutely nothing. Just be. I find a full body massage – with someone who doesn't hurt you! – to be an incredibly relaxing physical sensation. If you really have no money, have a spa session in your home. Run a hot bath and fill it with bubbles or salts, pour yourself a drink, grab some chocolate, light a few candles, and ease yourself and your book into the indulgence. Stay there until you turn into a prune.

9. Get out of town

You don't need to go far, but time away from your usual environment is often just the medicine. If you can't quite afford the Grandhotel Pupp in the Czech Republic, don't scoff at the wonderful and very affordable bungalows the South African National Parks (see www.sanparks.org) has to offer. The bush is one of the most phenomenal places when it comes to restoring the soul. I'm quite convinced that the deserts are my spiritual home. Whenever I'm in the Namib or Kalahari, I experience a tremendous sense of renewal – very different from the energy boost I get from London. You can find something closer to home, if needs be, with a minimum of effort. And don't be scared to travel on your own – it's enriching.

10. Get your hands dirty

My lovely friend (literally – she was Miss South Africa in 1984) Lorna Potgieter considers the nursery to be her best 'therapist'. When she's feeling down, she heads for the local nursery, buys a few trays of seedlings and spends the next few hours planting. 'Not only is it relaxing, but I soon find "me" again,' says Lorna. Many women experience the same pleasure in cooking or baking. It may well be that the absorption of your conscious mind in a fairly menial task gives your unconscious a well-earned break! I like to wander around the house straightening everything. Some may call it sad, or even obsessive-compulsive, but I call it meditative therapy.

11. Spend time with an animal

I mean the furry kind, although the party animal may not be such a bad idea. There is nothing more therapeutic than stroking an animal. My preference is dogs, but any warm little creature will do just fine. My dog Rufus is a real snuggle bunny – and he's a bull terrier! He takes his job of being my companion and protector very seriously and is able to sense when I'm feeling low. He comes over to me, rests his head in my lap, looks up at me with his soulful, triangular eyes, and my heart melts. If I'm snappy with him, the regret that immediately follows does help to rebalance my equilibrium. Did you know that extensive research has been done into the positive therapeutic effects of animals on people who are depressed, seriously ill, in jail or in any space where they are feeling really bad?

12. Photo albums

Digital is all good and well, but it is no substitute for physically paging through your photographs. Even though I keep my photos on my PC these days, I still print out a few snapshots for my albums. Looking at the ridiculous hairstyles, what-was-I-thinking? outfits, inappropriate men, fabulous places, wonderful friends and fun times is sure to lift your spirits – even if you have to have a good cry first. This may sound a bit loopy, but I like to touch the people or animals in the photographs. It creates a kind of bonding I can't quite explain. Don't scoff until you've tried it!

13. Read old love letters and greeting cards

Poring over old love letters and cards – even if they're from someone who turned out to be an A-grade asshole – is surprisingly uplifting. That someone thought all those wonderful things about you at some point is good for the spirit. Please tell me, though, that you are *not* keeping the cards and letters from the people who have really hurt you. This is bad energy, dear diva. If you do still have these letters and cards, have a ceremonial burning session. Chances are you will actually feel your spirit soar with the flames. Just don't burn down the house. A walk down memory lane is a great release, providing you choose the right lane.

14. Count your blessings

When you're in the dumpster, find somewhere quiet and warm to sit or lie, and count your blessings. You can even do it as you drift off to sleep at night. Write them down if you want, or list them in your head. Either way, you'll soon realise that you are one very lucky, very special person indeed. Besides friends, family, a home and so on, be sure to count the small things too – your eyesight, a daily hot bath, your dog or cat, your bed, the electric blanket, the feel of the velvet throw on your bed against your skin, sunflowers, whatever. The smaller the blessings you count, the more you are able to grasp how truly blessed you are. Do not allow any negative thoughts at this time – banish them as soon as they appear. If you're not able to meditate, this is a fantastic substitute.

15. Shopping

Another idea from the lovely Lorna. Shopping for groceries is not shopping with a capital 'S'. The shopping Lorna is talking about is shopping for spoils and treats, just because you can! Knowing Lorna as I do, she spends a lot more time shopping for other people than for herself, but the effect is the same. What you buy does not have to be high ticket – a few Charlotte Rhys soaps are a wonderful luxury. I love shopping in London. London recharges my batteries – there is so much vibrant energy there that I can't sleep. I walk and walk and shop and shop, and the mindlessness, the anonymity and the exercise all serve to take my mind off my troubles.

16. Ideas from men

I asked three of my favourite men for their input on what we women can do to lift our spirits when we're feeling blue. Here are their very diverse replies:

Chris van der Walt (and they don't come more yummy than this man):
- Spoil your body with sensuous things.
- Slow down – even your speech.
- Purposely erode some piece of nonsensical arbitrary authority.
- Be rude to a traffic cop.

Allan Meyer (now here's a man with a romantic soul):
- Find someone who truly loves you for who you are, then get away from your normal environment and talk only about one another.
- Bring back the memories of why you decided to do what you have done in your life and relive the positive sensations you may have lost.
- Remember that destiny is simply one's personal fulfilment, and if the blues set in, it could be a negative addiction that feeds on your discouragement. Discern the 'poor me' addiction and fight it with a vengeance. When you recognise the addiction for what it is, it won't be so ready to rear its ugly head.

Ashley Marchment (every girl needs a man like this in her life):
- Phone up an old flame and tell him that, years ago, he promised to take you away from all this, so how about meeting for a long Friday lunch instead?
- Go swimming with dolphins in Mozambique through Halo Gaia.
- Join a day-hiking club.
- Buy a talking parrot and teach it to swear.
- Take a Ferrari for a test drive.
- Go shooting at a range.
- Kickboxing classes will help you get rid of pent-up frustrations.
- Fill your garden with colour – get hundreds of silk flowers and plant them in your flowerbeds.
- Join a dinner-date group and, in just one night, meet at least twenty new people. Make up some intriguing stories about yourself, or learn to read Tarot cards and predict wonderful futures for everyone.
- Wear sexy silk knickers – no one will know except you.
- Cut out a photo of your favourite film star and walk around the shops with it in your knickers, facing inwards – again, only you will know.
- Hire a Harley-Davidson for a weekend and terrorise the folk in a one-horse town.

It is okay to wallow in self-pity or despair for a while, but agree with yourself on how long this should last. Pick a time frame you know is realistic, based on past experience of your lows. If your limit is one week, allow yourself one week of misery and then get on with it, whether you are feeling better or not. In this way you get to appreciate your blues without coming down on yourself, but you are also able to recognise when your low is a serious depression rather than the mild blues. Everyone gets depressed – this is normal – but if you find that you are chronically miserable more than once a month, consider getting professional help.

MUSIC, MOVIES AND BOOKS

> 'Even though I make those movies, I find myself wishing that more
> of those magic moments could happen in life.'
>
> *– Jane Seymour, (English actress; 1951–?)*

As I've said, I often disappear into music, books and films when I need a pick-me-up. I find it easy to free my emotions, be they anger, sadness or sheer misery, through these art forms. Whatever your formula for releasing your emotions, be careful of using other people as punch bags. Offloading is best done on one's own. Being able to work through your emotions or troubles on your own also helps to prepare you for the loneliness you'll find at the top of the corporate tree.

If you have no idea as to which – or even if – music, movies or books will work for you, feel free to try out mine. I've compiled a few lists to give you ideas, but do bear in mind that this is my list and you need to decide whether the subject matter is suitable for you or not.

Music

I love music. My favourite is noisy, driving rock. It is almost impossible for me to list even my 'Top 100' songs, but here is a list, in no particular order, that I think is the bee's knees. These always make me feel better:

1. 'Fisherman's Blues' by The Waterboys
2. 'Bring Me Some Water' by Melissa Etheridge
3. 'Rain King' (and 'Mr Jones') by Counting Crows
4. 'Holiday' by Green Day (and the cover by Hayseed Dixie)
5. 'Crazy On You' by Heart
6. 'Just Like Heaven' by The Cure
7. 'Hallelujah' by Jeff Buckley
8. 'The Mexican' by Babe Ruth
9. 'Refugee' by Tom Petty & The Heartbreakers
10. 'Rhiannon' by Fleetwood Mac

11. 'Flying Low' by Willard Grant Conspiracy
12. 'Rainin' In Paradize' by Manu Chao
13. 'Born to Run' by Bruce Springsteen
14. 'Killing Moon' by Echo & The Bunnymen
15. 'Maria' by Blondie
16. 'Candy' by Iggy Pop and Kate Pierson
17. 'Love Minus Zero' by Bob Dylan
18. 'Blaze of Glory' by Joe Jackson
19. 'Rebel Rebel' by David Bowie
20. 'Boys of Summer' by Don Henley

Movies

There's a whole book that is dedicated to using movies as 'self-medication' called *Cinematherapy: The Girl's Guide to Movies for Every Mood* by Nancy Peske and Beverly West. It's great fun, but they have the following to say about *Pretty Woman* with Julia Roberts: 'We've never understood the romantic appeal of a money-grabbing corporate raider taking up with a streetwalker he's hired to give him a blow-job.'

Well. I liked that movie! If you agree with them, buy the book, but here are my favourite movies for when I'm feeling sorry for myself or just downright blue. They are mostly 'chick flicks', but some are *skop, skiet en donner* (or 'dick flicks', as I heard them referred to the other day):

1. *Just Like Heaven* with Reese Witherspoon
2. *Last Holiday* with Queen Latifah
3. *The Butcher's Wife* with Demi Moore
4. *You've Got Mail* (and *Sleepless in Seattle*) with Meg Ryan
5. *Bull Durham* with Susan Sarandon (I have watched this more than twenty times)
6. *The Long Kiss Goodnight* with Geena Davis
7. *Double Jeopardy* with Ashley Judd (for when you're having revenge fantasies)
8. *Kill Bill 1 & 2* with Uma Thurman (as above)

9. *The American President* with Annette Bening
10. *America's Sweethearts* with John Cusack
11. *The Thomas Crown Affair* with Rene Russo
12. *Casino Royale* with Daniel Craig
13. *Die Another Day* with Pierce Brosnan
14. *After the Sunset* with Pierce Brosnan
15. *The Matrix* with Keanu Reeves
16. *Constantine* with Keanu Reeves (if you like your movies dark)
17. The *Back to the Future* trilogy with Michael J Fox
18. All the *Lethal Weapon* movies with Mel Gibson
19. All the *Harry Potter* movies
20. Both *Men In Black* movies with Tommy Lee Jones

Books

I have already recommended a list of books that have serious content, so for a little 'light reading', here are fifteen (and a bit of cheating) of my favourites:

1. *Eat, Pray, Love: One Woman's Search for Everything* by Elizabeth Gilbert
2. *The Battersea Park Road to Enlightenment* by Isabel Losada
3. *An English Psychic in Hollywood* by Lucinda Clare (the ending's a bit naff)
4. *Unreliable Memoirs* by Clive James
5. *Tuesdays with Morrie* by Mitch Albom
6. *The Emperor's Babe* by Bernardine Evaristo (unlike anything you'll ever read)
7. *Like Water for Chocolate* by Laura Esquivel
8. *The Secret Life of Bees* by Sue Monk Kidd
9. *E: A Novel* by Matt Beaumont
10. *Father Frank* (and *The Man Who Fell In Love With His Wife*) by Paul Burke
11. *The No. 1 Ladies' Detective Agency* by Alexander McCall Smith (and all the others in the series)
12. Anything by Tom Robbins (especially *Half Asleep in Frog Pyjamas* and *Fierce Invalids Home from Hot Climates*)

13. Anything written by Carl Hiaasen, the ultimate environmentalist and creator of the best fictional baddies imaginable, especially *Nature Girl*

14. Not to forget Wendy Holden for something light and frivolous

15. Jane Austen – she should be a compulsory inclusion on all lists

Enjoy and feel better.

LIFE LESSONS FOR THE WORK DIVA

'There is no easy or quick plan to happiness, there is no single spot where you can start. Where you are right now is the best place to begin. Be careless in your dress if you must, but keep a tidy soul.'
– *Samuel Langhorne Clemens, aka Mark Twain*
(American author; 1835–1910)

Much is said about the evil of the corporate world and the greed, rather than need, that motivates it. I'm sure this is all true, but corporations are an integral part of capitalism, and capitalism is the economic system that currently rules most of the planet. Companies create and destroy, are altruistic and avaricious, kind and cruel, nurturing and discarding. But the corporate world has no soul, so, like a vampire, it sucks its soul from the people it employs.

You can lose your soul without even realising it's gone. Did you see the movie *The Devil Wears Prada* with Meryl Streep (who plays Miranda Priestly – don't you just love the irony in that surname?) and Anne Hathaway (as Andy Sachs)? If you did, you will remember that Andy Sachs is seduced by the devil, in a manner of speaking, but manages to recover her soul in the end.

The corporate world is an exciting, yet potentially dangerous, world, so how do you make sure you enjoy the best of it without selling your soul to the proverbial devil? Here are twelve important tips on how to keep the devil at bay:

1. Don't lose your sense of self

When you lose your sense of self, you forget who you are – and I don't mean your name. You lose your identity in terms of what's important to you, your values, and your ability to relate to your friends and family – in much the same way as Andy Sachs did in *The Devil Wears Prada*.

As you climb the corporate ladder, you will change. You will learn and grow and expand your horizons, and all of this is good stuff. But you need to retain the essence of *you*. Go back to your 'good' list for a moment. There, in front of your very eyes, is the definition of who you are. Keep that list safe, and when you're feeling uncertain, haul it out and see how truly fantastic you are.

2. Your job will not love you back

No matter how much you love your job, it will not love you back. It has no soul, remember? If, heaven forbid, you were to experience an awful illness or loss, you would get flowers and support from the *people* at work, but not from your job. Sooner or later your job will say, 'It's costing me too much to pay a salary to a person who is sick (or in mourning or whatever),' and you will be unceremoniously dumped.

By all means, love your job by giving it your smartest and hardest work, but don't give it your soul. Your job is a fair-weather friend.

3. Accept failure as success

Don't get too despondent if you fail at something, regardless of whether this is a project, a job, a relationship or a company. Everyone fails at some point in their life. Hell, I have been (nearly) expelled, fired, called 'unemployable', lost all my money (twice!) and still managed to climb the ladder. I have learnt far more from my failures than from my successes, although the last time I lost all my money, I would have preferred to have spent it on a two-year residential Harvard MBA.

If you have faith, any kind of faith, you will understand what I'm about to tell you. I believe the reason I lost all my money is because of a lesson the universe wanted to teach me. At the time I got wiped out financially, I was chasing money rather than that about which I was passionate. Next minute – poof! – money gone. Although I was on the bones of my financial butt, the experience helped me to reclaim my soul.

4. Letting success not be your failure

We spoke a moment ago about not losing your sense of self. What I mean by not letting success be your downfall is: Don't become more important than yourself. Just because you succeed doesn't make you a better person than the next guy.

I learnt a valuable lesson in this recently when Simon and I were on the island of Rhodes, in Greece, with my folks. On the last day of our holiday, a fairly dishevelled taxi driver arrived to pick us up. He looked like a bit of an oik to me. Simon, being the friendly chap that he is, started chatting to the driver as we drove to the airport, and by the time our trip was over, we did not want to leave the cab. Taximan turned out to be a passionate amateur intergalactic photographer. He was the most fascinating, intelligent, well-read person I'd encountered in years. Another slap around the ears from the universe.

5. Knowing when to throw in the towel

When should you give up? When is it better to walk away? When should you stick it out through thick and thin? The answer to these questions, as with many other questions in life, is 'it depends'. You need to use your judgement. As I have said before, distinguish between when you need to walk away, and when you are making excuses for giving up because the going is too tough. If you throw in the towel too easily, you don't get to experience the enormous high of a hard job done well. The person who loses, if you give up too easily, is you.

If, on the other hand, you make the difficult decision to throw in the towel – whether this is on a job, a bad relationship, a poor investment or whatever – don't punish yourself. Giving up is a difficult thing to do, so the last thing you need is to beat yourself up too. Pick yourself up and dust yourself off – and be ready for the next round.

Do you know what the saying 'fighting the fights you can win' means? Try to figure it out – it will help you to judge when to walk away and when to stay and fight. A very useful book for you to read on this subject is *The Dip* by Seth Godin. It is subtitled *The Extraordinary Benefits of Knowing When to Quit (And When to Stick)* – and it's only eighty pages long!

6. Dealing with the bad times with dignity

On the subject of difficult times, life is going to come along and kick you in the teeth – especially when you are low. It is very easy to get self-righteous or adopt the victim pose when you get fired or retrenched or you miss out on that promotion on which you had set your heart. You can shout and accuse and blame, and if you know that this is how you usually deal with the low blows, take a close look at what this does to those around you – particularly your loved ones – and to your soul.

The temptation to lash out is sometimes overwhelmingly huge, and sometimes you *will* need to fight back, but there are just as many times when you have to accept defeat with dignity. Edwin Markham *(American poet; 1852–1940)*, best known for his poems of social protest, said, 'Defeat may serve as well as victory to shake the soul and let the glory out.' This can only be true if you don't become a howling banshee of some sort when times get rough.

7. Take criticism constructively

Most of us hate being criticised, even if the criticism is intended for our benefit, or if we have invited the input. Have you ever asked your partner if a certain outfit made your bum look fat, and when he told you that it did, you punched his figurative lights out? There are times when you are going to be criticised – whether to correct your behaviour, or give you discipline, or help you to improve – and you are not going to like it. What is the best way to deal with criticism?

Step 1 – be in the moment and listen. When someone criticises me, I tend not to hear properly because I am so busy preparing my counter-attack. Sit quietly and listen to what they have to say.

Step 2 – thank them for their input. This is very hard when you are saying, 'Oh, shut up, you bloody moron,' in your head, but be gracious and thank them anyway. Try not to verbalise anything other than 'Thank you for taking the time to bring this to my attention.'

Step 3 – think about what the person has said for *at least* one full day, preferably two or three. Be angry if you want, but then try to see if maybe, just maybe, they have a point. You can ask loved ones what they think, but if they agree with the person who has criticised you, you may end up being angry with two people.

Step 4 – respond to the criticism, if this is necessary. After thinking about things, you might find that your considered response will be very different from what your reflex response would have been.

Step 5 – if the criticism is valid, add it to your 'bad' list and let the behaviour go.

8. Strive to be a role model

The intention behind this point is not to massage your ego; it is to help you become more aware of your behaviour and the impact it has on others, and, in so doing, to help those around you. The higher you climb up the corporate ladder, the more people will watch your behaviour and want to emulate it. You can choose to be a role model – there are formal programmes (the UK has lots of them) and projects such as mentoring or coaching – or you become a role model without even being aware of people copying what you do, what you say or how you treat others.

Let's assume for a moment that people are drawn to you or admire you, and that you know you should be setting a good example. Where do you start? Let me ask you a question: Do you treat others as you wish to be treated? And I mean *all* others, including the waiters in restaurants and call-centre staff. If not, then that is where you need to start, and you will find that the rest follows.

The English author Samuel Johnson said, 'The true measure of a man is how he treats somebody who can do him absolutely no good.'

This, for me, is so true. Here's a piece of advice for nothing: If you want to know how a potential romantic interest will treat you, watch how he treats waiters. When your relationship hits hard times, as they all do, however he treats the waiters is how he will treat you. The reverse is true too, of course. If you are a little bitch with those in the service industry, this is what he can expect to receive from you. Dump the inner bitch and you will find your soul.

9. Be true to yourself

People go to war for what they believe – or are told to believe. Think of the Crusades, the Holocaust, apartheid. Do you know what you believe, or do you go to war for someone else's agenda? Values are passed from generation to generation and from corporation to corporation, often without any interpretation on the part of the recipients. Let's take a couple of simple examples. Why get married? Why have children? Is it because this is what is expected of you, or because it is what you want with the whole of your heart and soul? Be true to yourself, even if it flies in the face of convention.

Being true is difficult in the work environment, especially with business trying to steal your soul. It is even more difficult when what you believe conflicts with what others expect of you. *Freakonomics*, the fascinating book by Steven D Levitt and Stephen J Dubner, challenges the very essence of 'conventional wisdom', so if you need a little support for going against the system, read the book. It will also, incidentally, tell you why drug dealers live with their mothers.

Remember that I said that my marriage was 'a story for later'? Here's that story, but first, the background. I was raised according to fairly traditional standards. A woman went to high school, got a job, got married (no living together) and then had children. The End.

On with the story. Simon and I had been together for about three years when I moved in and he started proposing to me. He proceeded to propose to me at least once a week for the next ten years. My standard response was, 'Why do you want to ruin a perfectly good relationship?' I'd never imagined myself floating down the aisle in a white dress and wasn't too keen on the idea of having children. My passion, as I've said before, was the business world.

Time passed, stuff happened and I changed my mind about marrying Simon. I knew that marriage was important to him, and with what I had been through, my values had shifted. But I didn't tell Simon that I'd changed my mind. I had work commitments in Europe for the whole of January and February 2004. I'd seen Simon in London at the beginning of January, and we'd had a dirty weekend in Paris in early February, but other than that, we were apart.

In February 2004, I sent out individual text messages to all our friends, saying, 'I'll be back in Joburg end February. Won't have seen you for two months. Meet Simon and me for lunch at Casalinga on Sunday 29 February at 13h00.' I sent out another message to very close friends and family saying, 'I'll be back in Joburg end February. Won't have seen you for two months. Meet Simon and me at home for champagne at 11h00 on Sunday 29 February and we'll go for lunch.'

I arrived back in Johannesburg on 27 February 2004. Simon and I went out for dinner the next night and were still doing a conga line through the lounge of Michele and Maurice Kerrigan's house in the wee hours. At 07h00 on Sunday 29 February, Simon was greeted with a card, a cup of tea and Van Morrison playing 'Have I Told You Lately'. My sorely hungover man thought it was a belated Valentine's card, but inside it read, 'If you want to marry me, this offer is subject to the following conditions [you must bear in mind that I am a professional negotiator]:

1. It's today
2. You pay
3. I do want a ring and a honeymoon.'

Simon looked at me and asked, 'What do you mean, it's today?' I explained that if he wanted to marry me, a minister was coming to the house at 11h00 and we would get married. No pressure or anything – he could say 'no' if he wanted. Simon immediately phoned my father and said, 'John, your daughter has proposed to me. Can I say yes?' My father replied, 'Please, Simon, before she changes her mind.' Simon did not tell my father that he would be attending the wedding in a few hours' time.

Simon and I spent the next few hours writing our vows, finding something to wear (I was not presumptuous enough to buy a dress – I genuinely didn't want him to feel pressurised), scraping the icing off a beautiful Christmas cake we had forgotten to use the December before (only to find the 'Merry Christmas' of the red icing had stained the cake, so we then had to find a big statue to plonk on top of it, and convincing Dave Bensted-Smith, our extremely talented amateur photographer friend, to bring his camera, without letting on why he had to bring his camera along for champagne.

At 11h00, a small group assembled at our house for champagne. They knew that something was up when they saw that they were not the only ones at the house. The minister was ushered in, and Simon announced to our dear ones that they were, in fact, at a wedding. Five minutes later, we were married. The girls proceeded to drink, while the men – ex-military types – bawled their eyes out. And then we went off to lunch, where the rest of our friends – all deeply suspicious – were waiting. They started cross-questioning Simon as to whether I had proposed or not, what with it being a leap year and all.

Simon stood up to say his speech and announced, 'Yes, you are all quite right, Kim did propose to me,' at which point our dear friends started whooping and cheering. Simon shouted above the noise and the 'I knew it(s)', 'But wait, there's more.' The room went quiet. 'We got married two hours ago, so you're now at our wedding reception.' Cheering, drinking, tears and impromptu speeches. We both say it was one of the happiest days of our lives.

Now you understand why, four years later, we were in Paris celebrating our 'first' anniversary. But why do I tell you this story? Because it's about being true to yourself rather than to convention. Listen to your inner voice and be guided by what you want and what you believe, not what your family or friends or church or bosses tell you to do.

10. You are your job

This brings us to a very important point. If your job clashes with your values, you have a problem. Before we got married – and one of the reasons I was able to take that step – Simon and I attended a series of Insight courses. They were, without doubt, the most difficult courses I have ever done. During the second of the three pro-grammes, a philosophical discussion took place on whether you become your job, or, if you are doing a job you hate, does this impact your soul?

In simple terms, assume you are a debt collector going around town smashing kneecaps – can you separate yourself from your job? What about if you are an executive in a company you find morally bankrupt – are you then not morally bankrupt too? I'm sorry if this is going to come as bad news, but *you are your job*. I know first hand that being in a company with a culture that clashed with my values did taint me. As you are your job, make sure that there is alignment between your company or job, and the true you. You owe it to your soul to make a change if there is a clash.

11. Find joy in the little things

Your job is filled with the 'daily grind'. This you can't usually change, but if you are able to find moments of joy in the small stuff, like having a laugh with your kids or cuddling your pets or having a cup of tea with a friend, you can lift the whole day out of the loo.

Simon has a dog, a bull terrier named Daisy, who is the most joyous creature on the planet. She is an absolute handful, always up to mischief, but she finds delight in everything. Her enthusiasm is infectious. Daisy's greatest joy is having a bark at the people walking their dogs past our house at dusk. She starts pushing me around (literally – the chair in my office at home is on wheels) from five o'clock in the evening to open the door for her.

Actively look for the small stuff that brings you happiness – watching birds, stroking a dog, enjoying a fabulous meal, drinking a glass of exquisite champagne, hearing children laugh, telling a joke, cooking. Whatever brings warmth to your heart is perfect. A funny thing happens when you look for joy in the small things – you suddenly realise how very blessed you are and how much easier it is to cope with all the crap.

12. Be prepared to share

Generosity, to my mind, is the most important attribute of being human. You may see something else as being more important and that's fine, but for me, it is generosity. This is not necessarily generosity in a financial or material sense – it is being generous of heart, having a generous spirit, sharing. If you have the financial means, and try to help where you can, great, but generosity can be in the form of kind words, deeds, information or even thoughts. If someone walks into the office and they look great, tell them! If they look down, take them a mug of hot chocolate. If they need help moving and you have a suitable vehicle, help them move. But generosity must come from the heart – it can't be tarnished with resentment. If you are resentful about doing something, then it is an obligation, not an act of generosity. Don't confuse the two.

I find it much easier to be financially generous than generous with my time. This is probably because time has more value to me than money (learnt that lesson, didn't I?). I also know that I've learnt about being a woman in the workplace the hard way – you should see the scars on my back – and would like to share my lessons with other women. I needed to find a way to impart this to all the aspiring Work Divas out there while making the best use of my time. This book is my way of being able to share my experiences of climbing the ladder with you. Thank you for giving me this opportunity.

Chapter 14

THE WHOLE OF THE LADDER: STEP BACK AND REFLECT

LOOK HOW FAR YOU'VE COME

> 'You climbed on the ladder
> With the wind in your sails
> You came like a comet
> Blazing your trail
> Too high
> Too far
> Too soon
> You saw the whole of the moon!'
> – *Written by Mike Scott of The Waterboys*
> *(Scottish band,* This Is the Sea; *1985)*

As we come to the end of our adventures in the world of the Work Diva, let's step back and survey how much ground we have covered and what we have learnt along the way.

You are now armed with the tools you will need to help you succeed in the seductive world of big business. Here is a forty-point checklist you can use as a Work Diva's *aide-memoire* and guide.

1. Don't let go of your dreams

It is easy, as you climb the corporate ladder, to get despondent and lose sight of your dreams. If you find the climb is getting you down, step back for a moment and check that what you are doing is what you *really* want to be doing. If it's not, don't be afraid to change ladders. It might mean a little short-term pain, but it will be worth it in the long run. As the Electric Light Orchestra song goes: '*Accroches-toi a ton reve*' (Hold on tight to your dream).

2. Diva or doormat?

According to Picasso, there are only these two types of women. Are you making the conscious choice to be a diva? It really is up to you – this immense power is in your hands, so go out there and make divadom your reality. People see you as you see yourself – what did Eleanor Roosevelt say about giving other people permission to make you feel inferior? See yourself as a diva, and so will they.

3. Dump the victim attitude

If you are wallowing in self-pity and the unfairness of the world, dump the victim mindset immediately. Divas are not victims! Divas don't blame others – they count their blessings, no matter how hard the going gets. Divas have the world at their feet and the top of the ladder within their sight. They know that if they want to climb all those rungs, it is up to them to make it happen.

4. The 'good' and 'bad' list

Have you taken the time to draw up your 'good' and 'bad' lists? It is an investment in yourself that will pay the most wonderful dividends. And it's so easy. Just take a piece of paper, a small amount of time, a dose of honesty, mix it all together, leave it in a drawer and, in a while, a beautiful new you will arise. It's the easiest self-help recipe imaginable.

5. Don't lose your identity

Just because you become someone's employee, boss, lover, wife, mother or friend should not mean that you lose your own sense of identity. Be proud of being Johnny's mother – especially as Johnny is the smartest/cutest/most charming kid on the entire planet – by all means, but retain that inner spark that makes you exclusively and uniquely you.

6. Is it because I'm not a man?

Let go of the penis envy. Don't allow yourself to even think, 'If I were a man' – it's not going to help and is a form of victimhood. Big business is controlled by men. Deal with it. As a woman, you are blessed with a range of attributes and powers that will enable you to get ahead in business without a penis. Take these powers out for a run and remember, nobody can make you feel inferior without your permission.

7. Ten disadvantages vs eleven advantages

When we had a look at whether being a woman in business is an advantage or a disadvantage, we concluded that all we need to do is maximise our advantages and the resultant power enables us to be wicked Work Divas – in the good way, of course. Make the most of what you have got and let go of what you can't change, especially those stereotypes that keep you in a box marked 'WOMAN'.

8. Choose to choose to have kids

The days of women having to be barefoot and pregnant in the kitchen are well behind us. Yahoo! Seize this freedom and embrace it – and make the choices that *you* want to make. Part of this choosing is deciding on whether you want to have children or not. If your man wants kids but you are uncertain or don't want them, you need to deal with this conflict and not just succumb to his (or your mother's) wishes. If it all goes wrong, you'll usually be the one left holding the baby. Literally.

9. It's okay to choose between kids and a career

You do not become less of a woman just because you want to choose between being a brilliant mother and being a brilliant businesswoman. Is it not preferable to be great at one rather than trying to be brilliant at both and ending up mediocre? Choose whichever one you feel passionate about at that point in your life and you won't go wrong. Get lots of information and input to help you make the decision that is right for you.

10. Cut the Cinderella fantasies

Take responsibility for your own life. This does not mean that you have to give up hope of finding your very own Prince Charming; it just means that you shouldn't allow yourself to become dependent on anyone else for your emotional or financial security and well-being. With freedom comes responsibility, so it's up to you to look out for yourself. It's a step you will never regret.

11. Choose how far up the ladder you want to climb

Another important choice you will need to make is how far you want to climb up the ladder. If you decide to choose kids over career, be realistic about your climb – you may want to consider climbing the ladder a bit more slowly, or at a later stage. If you choose to put your career first, be realistic about your abilities and be prepared to make the investment in your personal growth and development – and the sacrifices – needed to get to the top.

12. Have a passion for the business world

Getting to the top does mean investments and sacrifices, so if you don't have a steamy hot passion for the business world burning inside you, you will probably not be prepared to make the requisite investments or sacrifices. Be honest with yourself about your motives for wanting to achieve success in the business world.

13. Learn, learn, learn

Hand in hand with your passion for the big bad world of business needs to come a passion for learning. The climb to the top will require you to know a lot about a lot of things, particularly business, and having even the slightest unwillingness to learn will halt your climb like nothing else.

14. Read, read, read

Integral to learning is the need to read. Reading, too, should become a lifelong love affair. Start with easy-to-read books, and you will find yourself progressing to the 'heavier' stuff in no time. Being considered 'well read' is one of the biggest compliments you can ever receive.

15. Mentors are cool

If you have not worked with a mentor before, you have already begun the process – you are, in fact, holding a mentor called *Work Diva*! You do, however, need to start developing people mentors pronto. These mentors will share their knowledge and guide you up the corporate ladder, in the same way a guide dog leads a blind person. They will help you to avoid (or deal with) many of the pitfalls and obstacles you are bound to encounter along your career path. Don't be coy in approaching mentors; just remember to respect their time and their priorities. They are the Work Diva's equivalent of getting a Harvard MBA for free! Avoid choosing personal friends or loved ones as mentors.

16. Know your behavioural style

Take the time to understand how you typically behave in the workplace. To help you order and analyse your behaviour, be prepared to take advantage of a little stereotyping. Are you an Expressive, an Amiable, a Driver or an Analytical? Understand the impact this has on the people around you – there is good and bad in every style. Be prepared to modify your behaviour – not your personality – in order to make the most of your interactions with your bosses, colleagues, etc. (and it works in your personal life too!).

17. Being an authentic *you*

Win an Oscar for being the real you. Even though you may be required to modify your behaviour or add to your 'good' and 'bad' lists from time to time, don't sell out on being an authentic you. You are the best you anyone can be!

18. Sisters are for support

Recognise that the sisterhood is a support mechanism. Sisters can guide you only up to a point. Choose them carefully – you want to avoid the witches and the bitches

– and don't forget to include some men too. Your sisterhood is part of your social network – you are who you know. The sisters do not make good mentors.

19. Ditch your inner bitch

Being called a 'bitch' is not a good thing in the business world. It may be mildly amusing if you're in school, but you need to leave your inner bitch behind when you enter the grown-up world. This, again, is a behaviour that does not serve you, so put it on the 'bad' list. Also, watch out for hanging around with known bitches – you can get a reputation for being a bitch just by association.

20. Say no to gossip

Part of ditching the bitch is saying no to gossip. Remember the Three Filters Test – if you say 'no' to the questions 'is it true' or 'good' or 'useful', don't pass on the information.

21. First impressions count

Whether you like it or not, first impressions matter – so you need to groom, dress and behave like a *bona fide* Work Diva. You can control first impressions, to a large extent, so make them go the way you want them to go by paying due care and attention to being 'classy and fabulous'.

22. Strut your stuff

Part of the impressions people will form about you is driven by your attitude. 'Behaving' like a Diva does not mean doing a Mariah Carey or Jennifer Lopez special. It means projecting an air of inner confidence and pride in being you, warts and all.

23. Support impressions with substance

Even if you create the perfect impressions, this must be supported by substance – credibility, delivery, consistency, industry, honesty, reliability, responsibility and, ultimately, respect. Here are the ten sure-fire ways to earn respect:

1. Under-promise and over-deliver.
2. Get things finished.

3. Be consistent.
4. Work hard *and* work smart.
5. Say what you mean and mean what you say.
6. Keep your word.
7. Tell the truth, despite the consequences.
8. Take responsibility.
9. Don't be afraid to make difficult decisions.
10. Treat others with respect.

24. Your communication style talks

The way in which you use communication – the things you do or don't say, the words you choose, the e-mails you write – says a lot about you and influences the perceptions others will have of you. It is another element of development that the Work Diva can control, so it is worth investing the planning time to make your communication – verbal and written – the best it can be.

25. Use your words carefully

The words you use have a major impact on those around you. The power in carefully chosen words is so immense that it can directly impact your success in getting what you want. Be aware of the influence your behavioural style has on the way you use words and make any changes to your words usage via your 'bad' list. The most powerful of all the words? If.

26. Watch the swearing

Remember the three rules of swearing?
1. Don't swear in the business environment. That way you can't get into trouble.
2. See Rule 1.
3. See Rule 1.

27. Ask questions and listen

Effective communication is a balance between talking, listening and watching, but you should be spending two thirds of a conversation listening. And listen – really listen – to what is being said. To help facilitate communication, ask lots of questions. Prepare questions for important meetings before the meeting.

28. Trust your intuition

Don't ignore your gut feelings, but, equally, don't rely solely on instinct. Listen to what your intuition is telling you and factor this into your decisions.

29. Being blocked from getting to the top

As you climb up the ladder, you will need to start making contact with the powers that be at the very top of the corporate tree. If your boss is preventing you from establishing these high-level relationships, i.e. he or she is a Blocker, you must have a strategy in place to get access to the top. The big bosses need to know who you are before they can consider you for any promotion or high-level projects.

30. Valid Business Case for Mr Big

Recognise that the power in an organisation usually vests with those at the very top of the tree. Firstly, don't be unduly scared of the big bosses – they are, after all, human too. Secondly, do not put your foot into the office of the top dog if you don't have a *Valid Business Case*. This means that you need to be able to talk to Mr Big about how whatever it is that you want to discuss with him will impact the organisation at a strategic level. Save the operational detail for management – executives are interested in the big picture.

31. Tread carefully with affairs of the office

The chances are quite good that you will meet the man of your dreams in the office, but office affairs always have consequences. Steer clear of the married men and your boss, and your life will be a helluva lot easier. If you do fall in love with the boss, be prepared for a ride so difficult that it will be easier for you to leave the company. Sleeping your way to the top is not an option – it catches up with you eventually.

32. Let out your inner fox and wily woman

We women are blessed with feminine wiles, so don't be afraid to let them out to play. It's fine to be sassy and sexy, but please draw the line at blatant seduction – it will serve only to get you into trouble. See 'Affairs of the office' on the previous page!

33. Handle harassment with care

If you are the unlucky recipient of an unwelcome overture, you need to be certain that you have done nothing to invite the harassment. This will help to ensure that you keep the power, if you decide to take action. Any impropriety on your part does not help your case.

34. Beware of alcohol in the workplace

Alcohol and the office are not a good mix. Drink with caution at office functions. While it is acceptable for the men to get wasted, the same latitude is not extended to the women. Hypocritical for sure, but that's the way it is. No drunk divas.

35. Don't feck up your career

You will work long and hard climbing the ladder, so you don't want to make any stupid mistakes and mess it all up. Here are the five mistakes women make that are guaranteed to damage their careers:

1. Bring your baggage to work – you need to dump your out-of-control emotions.
2. Sell out on secrets – keep confidences confidential.
3. Believe your own lies – here are the twelve most common:
   - I can't say no;
   - I'm no good with numbers;
   - I feel guilty because I've got so much;
   - I'm not good at sport;
   - I can't draw/paint/cook;
   - I can't lose weight;
   - I lack confidence;
   - I was a bad student, so I won't go far in life;

- I can't sell;
- I'm a hopeless negotiator;
- I've got a bad memory; and/or
- I'll lose my friends if I'm successful.

4. It's because I'm not a man – stop with the penis envy, already.

5. Networking is overrated – no it's not, so get a social life!

36. The price at the top is high

You need to be very sure that the top of the tree is where you want to be, because it is a high price you will need to pay to get there. Understand what is motivating your desire to get to the top and check, then double-check, that you are prepared to sell your life to the corporate world. Selling your life is what it requires to get to, and stay at, the very top of the corporate world.

37. A bowl of cherries?

As part of the exorbitant entrance fee to the top of the ladder, you have to demonstrate the following nine attributes, like it or not:

1. Lose the right to your 'rights'.

2. Be self-reliant.

3. Develop a strategic outlook.

4. Show you are a leader.

5. Delegate.

6. Make tough hiring and firing decisions.

7. Make decisions. Period.

8. Cope with conflict.

9. Anticipate the unglamorous side of the top.

38. Expect to sell your life but hang on to your soul

You will need to know how to deal with the difficulties you invariably encounter at the top. Developing your own recipes for lifting your spirits when you are low, and boosting your own ego when life is kicking you in the teeth, is important. You need resilience, a rhinoceros-like skin, tenacity and energy to survive in the corporate world.

39. Life lessons for the Work Diva

The corporate world has no soul, so it will try to suck soul from the people it employs. It is easy to lose your soul without even realising it's gone. Here are the twelve tips to make sure you hang on to your soul:

1. Don't lose your sense of self.
2. Your job will not love you back.
3. Accept failure as success.
4. Let success not be your failure.
5. Know when to throw in the towel.
6. Deal with the bad times with dignity.
7. Take criticism constructively.
8. Strive to be a role model.
9. Be true to yourself.
10. You are your job.
11. Find joy in the little things.
12. Be prepared to share.

40. A sense of achievement

The climb to the top of the ladder is difficult, exasperating, challenging, gratifying, enlightening, fun and a whole host of other things. In all of this, though, you need to feel a sense of fulfilment. If you are continuously wondering why you are climbing and finding it to be a real grind, stop and take stock. Maybe the corporate world is just not for you – or maybe the top of the tree is not really where you want to be. In taking stock, decide what you enjoy and pursue that, whatever it is. Life is too short to be continually miserable. Redeploy your climbing shoes if the corporate world is not for you.

TOP TIPS FROM A WISE WORK DIVA

'Advice is like snow; the softer it falls the longer it dwells upon, and the deeper it sinks into the mind.' *– Samuel Taylor Coleridge (British poet and philosopher; 1772–1834)*

We have already had wonderful advice from Brenda Bensted-Smith, CEO of Ad Talent, but as we come to the end of the book, it's time to grab a glass of something interesting, sit back and reflect on our journey up the ladder.

Here are twelve fabulous tips from Brenda for all the aspiring Work Divas out there:

1. See the bigger picture. Recognise your own limitations and don't be too proud to ask for help when you need it.
2. Take responsibility and be prepared to take the blame. Do not blame others.
3. To be successful, you need to be prepared to take risks and go out on a limb.
4. You will outgrow some friends and mentors. Don't be scared of the change.
5. Learn to listen, to make eye contact, to control fidgeting, to understand cellphone etiquette – they all count.
6. Know your industry inside and out. Try to get to the point where you become the spokesperson for your industry.
7. Know more than anyone that you compete with or to whom you are regularly compared.
8. Network, network, network.
9. Create yourself as the brand. Get to the point where you, and not your product, are what people are buying.
10. Find a balance between overselling and underselling yourself or your company and products. Sell with sincerity.
11. Retain your femininity and don't be scared to use your feminine wiles.
12. Keep your childlike qualities – avoid being too self-aware.

SINGING YOUR OWN PRAISES

'If one man praises you, a thousand will repeat the praise.'

– *Japanese proverb*

Have you ever thought about yourself as a product? I hadn't, until my friend Louise Chain (an executive coach in Australia) suggested to me recently that I consider marketing myself as a product. What exactly did she mean?

My thinking on the subject was intensified after I interviewed Brenda Bensted-Smith. Brenda suggests that women create themselves as a brand – that we get to the point where *we*, and not necessarily our company's physical products or services, are what people buy.

If you were a product that you had to sell to the business market, how would you package yourself? What end of the market would you chase – high-volume and low-cost (as in a commodity), or high-quality and expensive (a unique, differentiated product)? Corporations or entrepreneurs? Would you want to capture a large chunk of the local market, or a smaller slice of the global market? Would you want to be a household name or an exclusive item?

Here is an easy-to-follow, five-step process to make sure that you really understand the product called 'you', that you make the best of the product, and that it becomes the most sought-after product in your market.

Step 1: SWOT yourself

The first and most important part of marketing yourself as a product is to recognise what your outstanding strengths and attributes are vs those that are not your strong suit. I have already suggested that rather than trying to fix your 'weaknesses', you focus on and grow your strengths. It's being brilliant in a couple of areas that will make you stand out in the crowd, rather than being okay at lots of things. It is useful, however, to understand your limitations.

A helpful exercise to do is a personal SWOT analysis where you write down all your *S*trengths, *W*eaknesses, *O*pportunities and *T*hreats (using a diagram like the one on the next page). As you develop your list, be objective and honest – only you need to see it. You should be focusing on what makes your offering better than those around you. Your aim, after all, is to be an exclusive and differentiated product.

STRENGTHS	OPPORTUNITIES
1.	1.
2.	2.
3.	3.
4.	4.
5.	5.
6.	6.
7.	7.
8.	8.
9.	9.
10.	10.
WEAKNESSES	THREATS
1.	1.
2.	2.
3.	3.
4.	4.
5.	5.
6.	6.
7.	7.
8.	8.
9.	9.
10.	10.

When you understand your Strengths and Weaknesses, analyse what makes you different from, and stand out from, your competition – your Unique Selling Points (USPs). What would make someone choose you over your potential competitors?

Step 2: Identify your target market

Once you have recognised your strongest and most competitive qualities, decide on which market you want to target. Who would want to hire or promote someone with your capabilities? Make a list of all the people or companies you would like to work with or for, as well as the type of positions you want to hold. If one of your strengths is your ability to play in a team, to comply with best practice or understand political alignment, then you are undoubtedly well suited to working in a corporate or structured environment. If you are more entrepreneurial and see yourself as a mover and shaker or self-starter, then you may do very well in your own business and need to find a backer or funding.

The more specific you can be as to who you should be targeting and why, the more successful your marketing drive is likely to be. It is in identifying your target market that you make use of the Opportunities and Threats identified in your SWOT analysis. Look closely at what could hinder or stop your marketing campaign. Decide on a plan of action to maximise each Opportunity, and to address and overcome each possible Threat. Detail is important, so don't skimp on *how* you intend to achieve your action plan.

A good book to read on the subject of defining a market for yourself is *Blue Ocean Strategy: How to Create Uncontested Market Space and Make the Competition Irrelevant* by W Chan Kim and Renée Mauborgne. The book looks at how to create markets and is easy to apply to the product of 'you'.

Step 3: Packaging

After analysing your product and determining the target markets, take a long, hard look at the packaging of product 'you'. Do you have a high price tag (as in asking for a high salary or a senior position) but look like a bargain-basement special? What changes do you need to make to the presentation of your product? This, again, is a time for honesty. If you need input, don't be too proud to ask for help from someone you respect. Be sure not to get defensive when the person gives you feedback, as you are, after all, asking for constructive *criticism*. Make the changes and then hit the advertising and marketing trail.

If you have nobody to ask for this kind of input, you can self-evaluate. Imagine yourself entering a room for a panel interview or an important cocktail party. What impression do you make? What do people think of you when they see you? What do you want them to think? Do they see a porn star or hear your colourful language when you are applying for the job of head of a school? What do you need to change?

Step 4: Self-promotion

Now that you know what you have to crow about *and* where you want to be crowing, it's time to start promoting your product. Very few of us are lucky enough to have someone doing our marketing or advertising for us, so we have to rely on self-promotion to get noticed – because, if people don't know who you are, how can they possibly consider hiring or promoting you? There is a fine line between being an egocentric braggart and promoting yourself, but this is no time for false modesty.

It is possible to sell yourself without selling out on your humility – and humility is a fundamental trait for anyone at any stage of life. If you are able to demonstrate the USPs you represent – that is, the substance behind the product – you will be able to market yourself confidently while remaining humble. It is when you make false promises about your product that you stray into I-Specialist territory. The best way to illustrate the value in your product is to give examples of where or how your USPs have contributed to a business in some way.

There are many ways to self-promote that are not obnoxious or in your face. Here are a few ideas:

– Extend your social network by attending all the networking functions you can find.
– Get involved in organising events, parties, groups, clubs, etc.
– Write for any publications that will accept your articles.

- Do committee or charity work.
- Speak up at meetings and share your ideas.

As a woman, you have to work harder than a man at promoting yourself and establishing your credentials. When I present courses with my colleagues – most of whom are grey-haired (not necessarily older) men – they carry with them an unchallenged air of authority. I, however, have to labour that much harder to establish my credibility. I've experimented with this. I have used exactly the same format and content as my male colleagues to introduce myself at the start of a course, yet my knowledge and authority are unnecessarily challenged early on, while theirs is not! It is only when I do a hard-sell introduction that I can command the same degree of respect my male co-presenters elicit. And we don't just present to men. *C'est la vie,* I guess.

Step 5: Ongoing evaluation

Once your product hits the stores, so to speak, you need to be constantly evaluating the quality 'you' deliver. Is it still current, attractive and in vogue? Are your USPs still unique, or do you need to add more features? Is your target market the same, or should you be looking at an advertising and promotions campaign for a new, fresh environment?

To improve the quality of your product, you need to be prepared to learn from your mistakes and make changes in order to ensure that you continue to attract your target audience. Keep in touch with your market – make sure that they don't forget about who you are and the wonderful, unique contribution that only *you* can make.

According to www.goliath.ecnext.com, there are four types of people in the world:

1. People who watch things happen.
2. People to whom things happen.
3. People who don't know what is happening.
4. People who make things happen.

Make your world happen for you, dear diva, and it can become your oyster.

The End

'In the name of the best within you, do not sacrifice this world to those who are its worst. In the name of the values that keep you alive, do not let your vision of man be distorted by the ugly, the cowardly, the mindless in those who have never achieved his title. Do not lose your knowledge that man's proper estate is an upright posture, an intransigent mind and a step that travels unlimited roads. Do not let your fire go out, spark by irreplaceable spark, in the hopeless swamps of the approximate, the not-quite, the not-yet, the not-at-all. Do not let the hero in your soul perish, in lonely frustration for the life you deserved, but have never been able to reach. Check your road and the nature of your battle. The world you desired can be won, it exists, it is real, it is possible, it's yours.'   *– Ayn Rand (Russian-born American novelist, philosopher and writer; 1905 – 1982)*

References

BOOKS

Byrne, Rhonda. *The Secret*. London: Simon & Schuster Ltd, 2006.

Cannadine, David (ed.). *Blood, Toil, Tears and Sweat: The Great Speeches of Winston Churchill*. London: Weidenfeld & Nicolson, 1997.

Chan, W Kim, and Renée Mauborgne. *Blue Ocean Strategy: How to Create Uncontested Market Space and Make the Competition Irrelevant*. Boston: Harvard Business School Press, 2005.

Chin-Lee, Cynthia. *It's Who You Know*. San Diego: Pfeiffer & Company, 1991.

Covey, Stephen R. *The 7 Habits of Highly Effective People: Powerful Lessons in Personal Change*. London: Simon & Schuster Ltd, 1989.

Dowling, Colette. *The Cinderella Complex: Women's Hidden Fear of Independence*. London: Fontana Press, 1982.

Friedland, Linda. *Having It All*. Cape Town: Tafelberg, 2008.

Godin, Seth. *The Dip: The Extraordinary Benefits of Knowing When to Quit*. London: Piatkus, 2007.

Gray, John. *Men Are From Mars, Women Are From Venus: How to Get What You Want in Your Relationships*. London: Thorsons, 2002.

Jarski, Rosemarie. *A Word from the Wise*. London: Ebury Press, 2007.

Levitt, Steven D, and Stephen J Dubner. *Freakonomics: A Rogue Economist Explores the Hidden Side of Everything*. London: Penguin Books Ltd, 2005.

Littauer, Florence. *Personality Plus: How to Understand Others by Understanding Yourself*. Oxford: Monarch Books, 2004.

Miller, Robert B, and Stephen E Heiman. *The New Strategic Selling: The Unique Sales System Proven Successful by the World's Best Companies*. London: Kogan Page Ltd, 1998.

Orman, Suze. *The 9 Steps to Financial Freedom*. New York: Crown Publishers, 1997.

Porter, Michael E. *Competitive Advantage*. London: Simon & Schuster Ltd, 2001.

Salmansohn, Karen. *How to Succeed In Business without A Penis: Secrets And Strategies for the Working Woman*. Lincoln: iUniverse.com, 2006.

Schott, Ben. *Schott's Almanac 2008*. London: Bloomsbury Publishing PLC, 2007.

Shaw, Phil. *Extreme Ironing*. London: New Holland Publishers Ltd, 2003.

Truss, Lynne. *Eats, Shoots and Leaves*. London: Profile Books Ltd, 2007.

Tzu, Sun, and Thomas Cleary (trans.). *The Art of War*. Boston: Shambhala Publications Inc., 2005.

Williamson, Marianne. *A Return to Love: Reflections on the Principles of a Course in Miracles*. London: HarperCollins Publishers Ltd, 1994.

Wiseman, Richard. *Quirkology: The Curious Science of Everyday Lives*. London: Macmillan, 2007.

REFERENCE BOOKS

Encarta Concise English Dictionary. London: Bloomsbury Publishing Plc, 2001.

MAGAZINES, NEWSPAPERS AND ARTICLES

Get It Sandton/Rosebank, May 2008

International Herald Tribune, 21 September 2005. 'To Swear Is Human' by Natalie Angier

Men's Health, March 2008

O Magazine, July 2006. 'What I Know For Sure' by Oprah Winfrey

Sunday Times, 6 July 2008. 'Much More Than Just A Pretty Face' by Anton Ferreira

Time Magazine, 24 March 2008. '10 Ideas That Are Changing The World' by Vivienne Walt

www.board.jokeroo.com/battle-sexes/124381-if-women-had-penis-day.html. 'If Women Had a Penis for a Day' (origin unknown)

www.dailymail.co.uk/femail/article-1024304/Why-more-women-losing-custody battles-children.html. Updated 5 June 2008. 'Why more and more women are losing custody battles over their children' by Sadie Nicholas

www.dumblittleman.com/2007/10/meeting-with-boss.html. 'Ten tips for a successful meeting with the boss', written for Dumb Little Man by Chrissy of The Executive Assistant's Tool Box (See OfficeArrow.com)

www.highroadsolutions.com/xintheworkplace.pdf. 'The Ethics of Using Feminine Wiles in the Workplace' by Maureen Sanders

www.percepp.demon.co.uk/power.htm. 'The Power of Words' by Robin Allott. Paper for the Language Origins Society, Amsterdam, 1990

www.time.com/time/magazine/article/0,9171,974090-2,00.html. 'Office Crimes' by Nancy Gibbs

WEBSITES

www.amazon.com/Books-for-Communication-Self-Growth-Happiness/lm/4DPOLHOCE5VN

www.anvari.org

www.changingminds.org

www.csun.edu

www.en.wikipedia.org

www.encyclopedia.com

www.goliath.ecnext.com

www.goodquotes.info

www.health.discovery.com

www.howtodothings.com

www.ias.org.uk

www.iht.com
www.imdb.com
www.ioljobs.co.za
www.law-of-attraction-guide.com
www.listafterlist.com
www.mindtools.com
www.montana.edu
www.motivational-inspirational-corner.com
www.nonstopenglish.com
www.obesity.org
www.quirkology.com
www.quotegarden.com
www.sanparks.org
www.thinkexist.com
www.units.nhs.uk
www.urbandictionary.com
www.washingtonpost.com
www.yourdictionary.com

Do you have any comments, suggestions or
feedback about this book or any other Oshun titles?
Contact us at **talkback@oshunbooks.co.za**